Gould Evans Affiliates

The Creative Spirit

Preface by Terry Richey
Foreward by Stephen Grabow
Introduction by Robert Gould and David Evans

Editorial Director USA
Pierantonio Giacoppo

Chief Editor of Collection
Maurizio Vitta

Publishing Coordinator
Franca Rottola

Graphic Design
Studio CREA, Milano

Editing
Martyn J. Anderson

Colour separation
Litofilms Italia, Bergamo

Printing
Poligrafiche Bolis, Bergamo

First published
January 2001

Copyright 2001
by l'Arca Edizioni

ISBN 88-7838-080-6

Gould Evans Affiliates

Contents

The Idea Firm

by Terry Richey

Terry Richey is a journalist, designer, and strategist. He runs Timberline Strategies, a long-range marketing think tank, from Santa Fe, New Mexico.

This book celebrates ideas. If you appreciate imagination, creative problem solving, and intriguing solutions, you will find many examples here. At Gould Evans Affiliates, ideas begin with a point of view and grow from a foundation of knowledge; they give life to the ordinary and shape to the future.

Perhaps no more visible palette for ideas exists than in design. Few architecture and design firms apply their ideas as deftly to their work as Gould Evans Affiliates. These are ideas that honor the traditional, in restoration and adaptive reuse projects; ideas that define new ways to think about a site, a building's purpose, and new materials; and ideas that change the way architecture itself is practiced.

What may be the most surprising quality of Gould Evans is not that they solve problems in unexpected ways or create beautiful buildings and landscapes. The surprise comes from how deeply ingrained the search for "the idea" is, and how this search shapes the work of everyone in the firm. An environment exists within the organization that encourages questioning, insights, and interaction—so much so that even the firm's walls, files, and furniture are on wheels to facilitate spontaneous teaming and open communication. This democratization of ideas challenges many traditions and assumptions about how architecture should be practiced. It has also contributed to the extraordinary growth of the firm.

Pulling the entire firm into the search for ideas is unusual. Completely integrating clients into this process is unique. Gould Evans Affiliates practices a clearly defined approach to design with heavy client participation. Client involvement takes place on many levels throughout the project, but most intensely during Gould Evans Affiliates' design workshops, also called charrettes. During a several-day retreat, a team that includes the clients and designers searches for approaches to the project. These dynamic, extensive workshops are part strategic planning, part problem solving, part design, and always productive. By the end of the retreat, the client's ideas are deeply embedded into the solutions. This, too, has contributed to the firm's strong growth.

The architecture practice appears to be evolving from a traditional parochial model in which local firms provide self-contained, services, to an environment of collaboration and partnering between firms and disciplines. The next step in this evolution is the designer as thought leader serving in a broader and more integrated role with the client.

Gould Evans Affiliates seeks to provide insights of value on every project it undertakes. For the client, those insights translate into ideas that reduce costs, improve functionality, enhance design, protect resources, and create beauty. For society, it means showing again and again that design has the power to make things better.

Architecture As Place

by Stephen Grabow

Stephen Grabow is Professor of Architecture and Urban Design at the University of Kansas. He is the author of Christopher Alexander: The Search for a new Paradigm in Architecture *and numerous essays on the relationship between architecture, art, and science.*

The buildings and projects of Gould Evans Affiliates represent the results of the firm's continuing search for holistic, unifying design concepts that create a deep-seated, almost archetypal sense of place. This search reflects the ideals of the founding principals, Robert E. Gould and David C. Evans, whose architectural education was formed in the second decade of the post-war period of modernism—when theorists and practitioners focused on humanizing the minimalism of the so-called International Style.

In 1951, the International Congress of Modern Architecture had developed a set of principles for combating the early signs of urban decentralization and suburbanization. They encouraged architects worldwide to focus their attention on the urban core, the "heart" of the city and, above all, on re-creating the strong "sense of place" that had characterized the buildings and spaces of architectural history. In the 1960s, these principles were expanded by a younger generation of modernists, the so-called Team Ten, to include a focus on re-creating community structures as well as urban institutions.

In 1961, Kevin Lynch wrote *The Image of the City*, which outlined the cognitive elements that make up our perception of urban place (such as paths, nodes, landmarks, districts and edges). At the same time, Gordon Cullen, in *Townscape*, developed the idea of pedestrian-oriented "serial vision" to combat the vehicular-oriented scale that characterized so much of the new development during the post-war building boom of the 1950s. And in *Community and Privacy*, Serge Chermayeff and Christopher Alexander developed a strategy for "a new architecture of humanism" based on a highly differentiated system of interconnected, pedestrian spaces that seemed vital to sustaining community life. At a conceptual level, Christian Norberg-Schultz developed the idea of spatial *"schemata"* and *genius loci*, or "spirit of place"; and Alexander, in *A Pattern Language*, catalogued the rapidly disappearing archetypal patterns of form that have historically given the environment a "timeless" sense of place.

As one looks at the buildings and projects of Gould Evans Affiliates and reads the designers' descriptions of their own work, there emerges a strong connection to this tradition of architectural thought in their search for a "sense of place" within the context of contemporary and sustainable materials and methods of construction. The ingredients of "place," as they emerge from that search – and from an analysis of the projects that are illustrated and described in this volume – are both physical and social; that is, they demonstrate the use of formal, geometrical ordering systems to create community structures within each building. Wholeness, or unity of form, the articulation of a central space or core, human scale, and a strong relationship to the contextual landscape combine with a ceremonial and symbolic use of space to create an arena or stage upon which the activities of the building are played out.

We find microcosms of cities and villages, for example, in the interior of the Central Resource Library, Beth Torah Synagogue, Prairie Elementary School, Court Avenue Station, and in Westport Corporate Center, with its systems of "project centers" that embodies its operating methodology. We see a diversity of adaptation to site and context by comparing the Cathedral Social Hall in Kansas City, the Language and Communication Building at Scottsdale Community College in Arizona, and the National Hurricane Center in Miami.

In all these projects, icons, beacons, or lanterns serve as landmarks that lead to entries, gateways, or portals. Corridors, arcades, promenades, and interior streets create wayfinding systems of spines and axial threads that lead to interconnected spaces, neighborhoods, clusters, pods, or courtyards. These in turn are organized around a perceived heart or hub that takes the form of a village commons, town square, forum, or central plaza that acts as or gathering place for social interaction and communal experience. Throughout, views, transparencies, and indoor-outdoor relationships serve to blend or dissolve the buildings into the landscape and root them in "place."

These ordering devices constitute the

archetypal language in which the design ideas or concepts are formulated. Each is an analog of some fundamental means of placemaking that illuminates the use to which the building is put. This language, in turn, becomes the means by which the interdisciplinary team members of Gould Evans Affiliates communicate with each other and with their clients.

Form-based, or morphic, analogs are organizational structures in the human mind that link us to space. They represent formations in the archetypal structure of the mind that correspond, isomorphically, to the material forces at work in the creation of human artifacts as well as to the dynamics of human experience. As such, they are powerful creative tools in the art of placemaking and we see them used consistently in many of the firm's buildings and projects. In the J.A. Rogers Middle School, for example, the building forms a stage on which the period of "transition" represented by the grades between elementary and secondary school is played out in both the internal spatial structure and the external geometry of the building form.

Modern architecture appears to have arrived at a crossroads. The minimalist functionalism of the International Style has been criticized for its narrow, mechanistic definition of human needs derived from the industrial assembly line, for lapsing into symbolic representation without satisfying human needs and requirements, and for ignoring site and context. Today, post-modern, deconstructivist, and *avant-garde* theorists and practitioners reject the functionalist premise of modern architecture—indeed, of modernism itself—on the grounds that it celebrated cold efficiency, rational organization and an aesthetic of inhuman machinery in the service of a bland and uniform technocracy. Rather than responding to the social commission of clients and users, much of what passes for contemporary thought at the turn of the century has become predicated upon pushing aside the functional and utilitarian dimension of architectural form in favor of a sweeping cultural critique. As the Finnish architect and scholar Juhani Pallasmaa observes, "the architecture and art of the closing decade of the second millennium have become so self-referential, so concerned with their own existence and self-definition that today art seems to be about works of art instead of being about the world, and architecture about buildings, not about life."

Pallasmaa sees this rejection of the functional and utilitarian dimension of architecture as a kind of *fin-de-siècle* nihilism in which the moral authority of great art is called into question while pressing social problems remain ignored. He argues for a new, ecological understanding of functionalism based on meeting fundamental human needs with an economy of expression in which the building is seen more as a living process rather than a product, on the priority of performance over representation in which metaphorical expression and practical craft are fused, and on adaptation to site and a return to the aesthetics of placemaking.

Buildings that strive to meet these criteria are ultimately about the life inside, not just visual images. The aesthetic appeal of architecture cannot be exclusively visual. Aesthetics is rooted in a much deeper realm of human experience than the dynamics of visual perception. As the philosopher Susanne Langer has so keenly observed, it is the entire realm of feeling that is encompassed by great art, and the form of feeling—the morphology of sentience—is the medium through which artistic creation occurs. In architecture, this requires an aesthetic sensibility with regard to the life that occurs in the building and is dependent upon a thorough understanding of the client's needs as well as a humane desire to improve the institutions of society. In the search for a new, ecological functionalism, the use of morphic analogs by Gould Evans Affiliates to create a deep-seated sense of place constitutes an exemplary signpost to a richer environment.

The Creative Spirit

by Robert Gould and David Evans

This book is about the beginning—the first 25 years of work from an architecture firm whose members have come together around a common belief in the art and the business of architecture. With a creative spirit expressed in an organizational culture that values our greatest assets—clients and associates—this belief is translated into how we practice and what we create.

Focus on the Client

The creation of quality architecture begins with superior client service. Service is a given; architecture is the goal. Only the limits of time and talent can keep us from achieving both in every project. Each project is an ongoing, interactive dialogue with clients, where alternatives are presented and evaluated on the basis of overall costs and benefits. This has allowed us to provide— and become known for—small-firm services backed by the vast resources of a large general-practice organization.

It is especially clear at this quarter-century moment that enduring client relationships continue to be critical to our growth and evolution. A two-decade relationship with the State of Kansas began with a major renovation of Marvin Hall, home to the university's School of Architecture and Urban Design. This project was a turning point for the firm and has led to a range of projects at campuses throughout the United States. A long-standing relationship with the Johnson County Library System has allowed our design teams and their leaders to test the limits of what a library can be to its community and how its technology and form interact.

Client decisions about firm selection can —and sometimes do—come down to a flip of a coin. Recognizing this, we have always made a major effort to distinguish ourselves early on by developing the client relationship and understanding the project before selection. We've always seen marketing as an opportunity to listen to and communicate with clients. It's the beginning of a mutual education process between the clients and our team. Engaged marketing is the first step toward the client interface that results in superior service.

Empowered to obtain and undertake the work, people within our organization push us to reach for the next level—of design excellence, project size, building type, and client expectation. Expanding our network of affiliates with design professionals who agree with our ideas about client service and marketing has made firm building invigorating and rewarding. Affiliate offices that grow with these ideas at their core have proven energetic and durable over time.

Teaming toward Solutions

Design by team is a fact of life. We are inherently smarter than any *one* of us. Ownership of ideas is never as important as their quality when better design is the goal. Since the earliest moments of our firm we have employed a team approach and utilized a highly inclusive workshop process to elucidate the greatest insights about every project that's on the board—or in the computer.

Our highly articulated workshop process, has become a signature of our firm. Connecting and collaborating with the client, user groups, other design disciplines, and every component of our own design team yields the greatest number and highest quality of concepts relating to any design or planning project. And project efficiency—an important aspect of client service in these speed-sensitive times—is enhanced by our workshop process.

There are many excellent solutions to any given design or planning problem. As a part of our process, we remain open to meaningful alternatives during the life of the project. Introducing a series of solutions at the workshop stage—including some that might appear contradictory—is critical so that these can be fairly evaluated by all members of the design team, especially the client and people who will work, live, or play within the context of the project.

Essence and Architecture

Our intentions in architecture go beyond shelter; we strive for a greater concept and purpose. Appropriate design—what is "right"—is situational, flexible, and a celebration of life with all its diversity, joy, and sadness. No esoteric dogma can drive this design process. Instead, the collective creative spirit is directed toward expressing an idea or unifying concept; comprehensively and honestly addressing all aspects of a project, and considering the project's reuse and recycling possibilities. Tackling these three areas has allowed us to create work that embraces its physical, social, and aesthetic potential while seeking to make a real contribution to our clients' needs and the built environment.

For us, it has never been about a signature style. Place and context have been guiding forces. Though we have significantly wider footing now, our firm originated and grew in the Midwest and remains imbued with a kind of Midwestern pragmatism. This manifests itself in our dual focus on design excellence and superior user-friendliness. This regionalism has, in fact, empowered our approach to firm building. As the Midwestern affiliates have always done, the newer offices push the boundaries of design excellence while paying heed to the issues of context. In Phoenix, for example, design teams use the region's desert climate, indigenous materials, and state-of-the-art technologies to create an architecture that is definitively of its place as it explores the edges of contemporary design.

Each project reveals, at some point, its unifying concept. This concept rises to the top over the life of every project, and it's one that all participants fully embrace and that pulls all elements of the project together. At the National Hurricane Center in Miami, for instance, a celebration of technology was the central idea that drove the design from start to finish.

Our teams adopt a comprehensive, holistic approach, addressing the physical, environmental, and material aspects; the social and institutional aspects; and the mystical or spiritual aspects that give the projects lasting meaning. At the J.A. Rogers Academy of Liberal Arts and Sciences, we used geometry as a way to depict the duality of science and art and create a place that would feel important to students and teachers.

Sometimes there is great value to be found in what's already there. Reusing an existing structure is often narrowly perceived as a less glamorous approach but it is highly

sustainable, an important consideration for many clients and communities. At Westport Center, one of our own affiliate offices found a home in a former retail complex made up of three historic buildings. This approach was pioneered in our Nickel Building offices in downtown Lawrence, Kansas, and has been emulated by affiliates ever since.

We have been through the start-up phase, the survival phase, and the growth phase. We are now in our mid-twenties, looking at the world of architecture and planning with great anticipation. Each project in this volume represents the trust our clients have placed in us, each is imbued with a powerful central idea, and each aspires to meaningful architecture. In the next quarter century, we aim to use every tool available to us—more diverse and creative teams, digital technology, new materials and systems—to surpass client expectations with design.

The world may be changing at a phenomenal rate, but we continue to work as Earth's short-term tenants with the simplest of missions: creating appropriate, quality places for people.

Works

J.A. Rogers Middle School

Kansas City, Missouri

The J.A. Rogers Academy of Liberal Arts and Sciences is a new middle school built on a wooded site that offered substantial grade change and dramatic views. The arts and sciences middle school is part of the Kansas City, Missouri, School District's magnet school system. Together, the client and the design team explored the question, "What is a middle school?" The dominating concept, they determined, is transition. The sixth, seventh, and eighth grades are the end of a child's total dependence on others and the beginning of responsible adulthood. At this critical time, the environment can be an important factor in the development of the individual.

The team created a design that symbolizes the youths' transitional struggle as well as representing the duality of science and art through the juxtaposition of a cylinder and a rectangular box. Geometry rules this environment, but art is the by-product. The two shapes seem to be absorbing each other, yet they are frozen in a transitional state. This formal interlocking is extended to the surrounding area. Extensions of the cardinal points of the modernist fountain in the adjacent park and a communications tower less than a mile from the site intersect at the hub of the new middle school, further bringing art and science together.

The clients and design team also wanted to emphasize the mind/body connection, and the connection of the students and their activities to the landscape. The cylinder is not complete, and in the wedge left open, the site rises up to the building. From inside, this wedge forms a viewing portal to the sports fields. Throughout the school, orientation to the landscape is emphasized by framed views. In the corridors, pre-cast columns act as locator devices that indicate a one's position within the structure (and on the site). These act as organizing elements that establish order and give clues to the methods of construction.

The rectangular form houses the public functions of the school at the neutral and easily accessible middle level. The collision of the rectangular volume and the cylinder creates a centralized crater, where the learning resource center is located.

The remainder of the cylindrical part of the building is organized into "learning families" and grouped around this hub of knowledge. A family is made up of the four disciplines (math, English, history, and science) in addition to various specialty classrooms.

The division of grade levels onto separate levels of the building addresses the adolescents' varying needs for security and their dual but conflicting need for acceptance by others and a chance to express their individuality. The sixth grade families occupy the lowest level, have the greatest degree of enclosure, and are the most isolated; they also have the strongest connection to the landscape. Students in the seventh grade, considered the search-and-discover year, are located on the center and most active level. In the eighth grade, the students rise above the common areas and share a floor only with administration. Here, they experience great freedom to develop their own interests and enjoy the best views.

The forms and the materials that further distinguish them work together to create a playful exterior with easily identifiable and accessible entry points. The design team felt that by articulating the middle school's mission, they could also create a dramatic teaching tool that could be included in lessons about math, science, art, and humanities.

Intersecting volumes and bold colors provide visual interest and navigability. Exterior walls punctuated with openings create portal spaces between interior and exterior and emphasize the building's connection to its site.

A – ENTRY PLAZA
B – BUS DROP-OFF
C – PARKING
D – ENTRY
E – OUTDOOR AUDITORIUM
F – CROSS COUNTRY TRACK
G – TENNIS COURTS
H – 100 METER TRACK
I – SOFTBALL FIELD
J – SOCCER FIELD

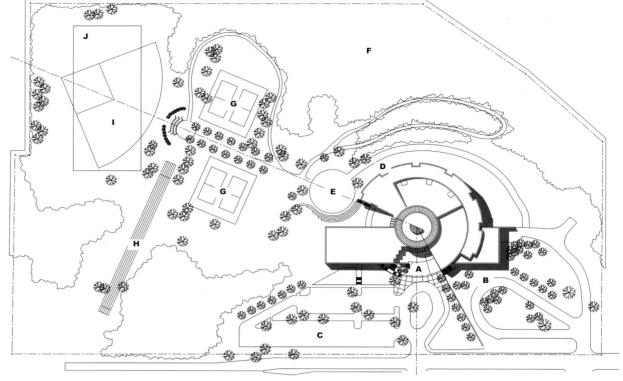

1 – OPEN TO BELOW
2 – ADMINISTRATION AREA
3 – VESTIBULE
4 – ENTRY
5 – PROJECT DISPLAY
6 – VOCAL MUSIC
7 – CONTROL ROOM
8 – PRACTICE ROOM
9 – OFFICE
10 – SEMINAR/SPECIAL
       EDUCATION
11 – INSTRUMENTAL MUSIC
12 – COMPUTER LAB
13 – MATH/SCIENCE
14 – RESTROOM
15 – HUMANITIES
16 – MULTI-PURPOSE LEARNING
17 – TEAM PLANNING/
       OBSERVATION
18 – APPLIED TECHNOLOGIES
       LAB
19 – ART
20 – DARKROOM
21 – PROJECT DISPLAY
22 – STORAGE
23 – LOCKERS
24 – MEDIA CENTER
25 – GYMNASIUM
26 – CAFETERIA
27 – STAGE
28 – FOOD SERVING
29 – KITCHEN
30 – LEARNING RESOURCE
       CENTER
31 – CONFERENCE ROOM
32 – TEACHER RESEARCH
33 – TRANSITIONAL CLASSROOM
34 – LANGUAGES
35 – SPEECH/DRAMA

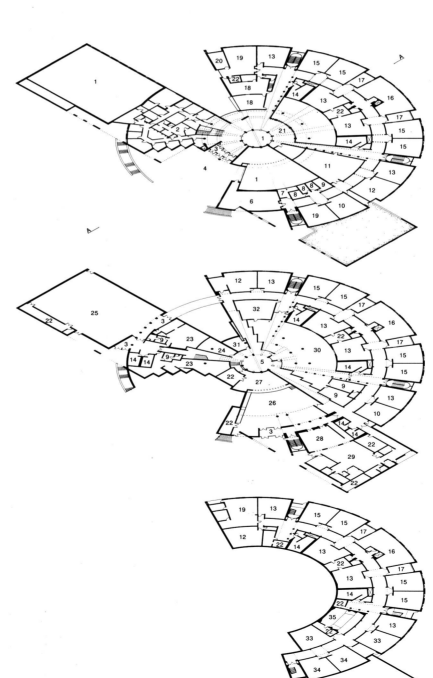

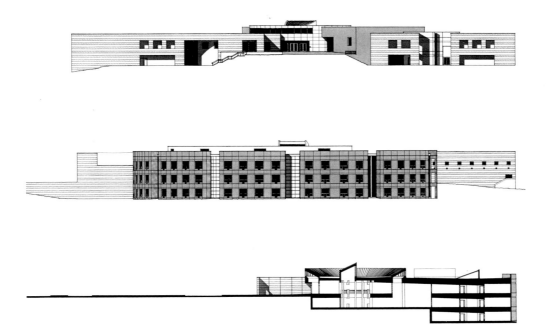

The exploded conceptual drawing, below, shows the layers of the building, the cylindrical core, and the concrete columns (which appear here as pins through the structure) that are used as locating devices within the structure. Sections, left, articulate the contrasting volumes of the building. In plan, opposite, these volumes appear as a partial circle overlaid with a rectangle. The wedge left by the incomplete cylinder and the rectangular volume shows clearly in the site plan, opposite top; this gap offers views of the playing fields and wooded setting.

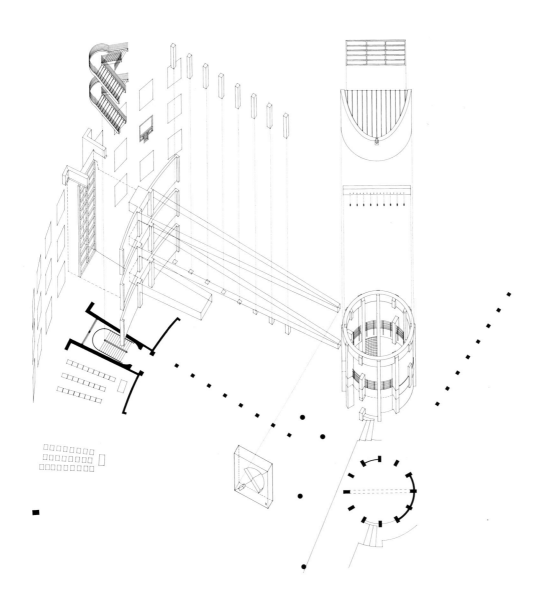

Part of the inner core of the cylindrical volume of the structure contains the learning resource center, opposite. Daylight brightens this dramatic space, which is configured to offer a variety of study options to groups and individuals. Stairs up to the gymnasium, left, draw the eye to the cylinder's innermost core, below. This atrium space was designed with hardware that would permit exhibit display from artwork to much heavier items such as a motor or a small car, as related to classroom studies.

Center for Health Education

Phoenix, Arizona

GateWay Community College's new Center for Health Careers Education is located at a prominent corner of campus and alongside one of the primary vehicular gateways into downtown Phoenix. The 76,000-square-foot building is comprised of laboratories and medical classrooms designed to simulate health care environments. It is a mirror image of a fully functioning hospital.

Many of the lab spaces needed to take full advantage of available wall space for storage and equipment. Some spaces needed to function without the disturbance of natural light. Instead of dispersing faculty offices adjacent to their respective teaching spaces, the building committee expressed the desire to integrate offices in one location to foster interaction among faculty.

The building design reacts to these challenges by exploiting the inherent nature of the design problem. The building is L-shaped in plan addressing its two prominent street edges. It is predominantly a masonry building with a large double height lobby that carves through the building, connecting the main entry with flexible outdoor spaces beyond. As a counterpoint to its mass, a glass and aluminum two-story wing of faculty offices shifts forward to take full advantage of distant mountain views. Necessary sun protection is celebrated on the exterior of this east facade through a suspended aluminum sunscreen. A faculty workroom expressed as a triangular wedge is an anomaly to this highly rationalized sunscreen. It cantilevers from the building and is shaped to take advantage of views to Camelback Mountain. Horizontally and vertically proportioned windows are punched into masonry wall bays, which themselves are based on the rhythmic proportions of the sunscreen. At night, the building glows from seemingly random slots of light. The entry lobby becomes an illuminated beacon, serving as a welcoming sign for nighttime use.

The sunscreen incorporates standard aluminum extrusions and custom bent aluminum plates. A series of horizontal louvers and vertical fins screen the offices from extreme sun angles. In plan, its panelized bays, whose dimensions are based on a typical office module, are shifted north out of alignment with office partitions allowing the vertical fins to not obstruct northeastern views to Camelback Mountain. It is hung off of the building, suspended above finish grade, and coordinated with a standard aluminum window system. The resulting composition celebrates the accumulated layering of these systems.

This project and the master planned campus are monitored and run on an energy management system. Controls, located at the central plant for the site, initiate startup and night shutdown procedures for each building on site. Each room within the building is monitored by sensors that actuate dedicated fans and lighting upon entry into the room. Low-water, indigenous landscaping provides shade in many exterior areas. Precipitation is retained entirely on site, providing erosion control and mitigating irrigation requirements. The design team has limited volatile organic compounds (VOCs) to help ensure the quality of indoor air.

The building plan created the opportunity for several multi-use outdoor spaces. A large amphitheater, indigenous and medicinal plantings, and a variety of seating situations set the stage for student interaction. A series of low retaining walls dissolve the building mass into the landscape. A charcoal, polished concrete block wall emerges from the lobby and cantilevers above the landscape. The transparency between inside and outside allows the lobby space to become part of the desert garden.

A masonry mass creates a
dramatic counterpoint to
the glass-clad office wing,
on which an aluminum
sunscreen is suspended
to limit harsh rays and
preserve views.

The L-shaped building includes laboratory and classroom spaces, faculty offices, and support areas. The configuration of the building on its site allows for outdoor spaces to be optimized.

SITE PLAN

1 – NEW CENTER FOR HEALTH EDUCATION
2 – AMPHITHEATER/DESERT GARDEN
3 – PEDESTRIAN PROMENADE
4 – DAYCARE FACILITY
5 – EXISTING EDUCATIONAL INSTRUCTION BUILDING
6 – PARKING

GROUND FLOOR PLAN

1 – MICROBIOLOGY AND CHEMISTRY LABORATORIES
2 – RESPIRATORY LABORATORIES
3 – TIERED LECTURE HALL
4 – LOBBY
5 – ADMINISTRATION
6 – FACULTY OFFICES
7 – HEALTH CARE UNIT

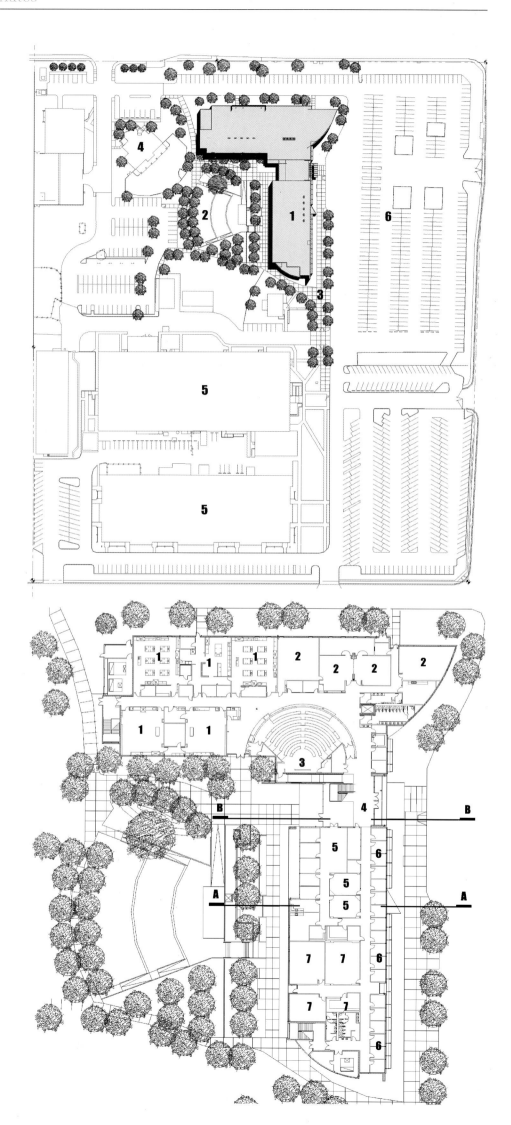

The Faculty workroom
space at night highlights
the building's transparency,
revealing internal accent colors.

The faculty office wing, opposite, features an aluminum sunscreen, which adds a sculptural element to the building volume and ensures that mountain views will not be obstructed, although direct sunlight is blocked.

A cantilevered masonry sheer wall serves as a link between the outdoor garden and the inside space, left. The facility includes a large teaching theater, and a double-height entry space and public stair, below; the ground floor of this space serves as a gathering area and transition zone to the garden.

Central Resource Library

Overland Park, Kansas

The new Johnson County Central Resource Library was designed to replaced an outdated and undersized main branch library and technical services facility.

Gould Evans Affiliates' unique charrette process—a highly articulated interactive design workshop—was utilized on this project to great effect. During the workshops, the teams (designers, clients, and others) extensively explored a number of important goals for the building. The client wanted a building that would be easily accessible and navigable for all; would express its function; would illuminate a new image (both "soft" and high-tech) for the institution; would be patron-friendly, service-oriented, and comfortable; and would be a "workhorse" facility with a strong civic presence.

The design team and the client were intrigued by the possibilities of reusing an existing structure, which would make financial and environmental sense. Because of the public nature of this facility, demonstrating the architectural possibilities of reuse seemed particularly attractive. A humble structure, a former retail "box," was acquired; its embodied energy and resources required to build new were preserved. In addition, on-site reuse of steel and concrete resulted in the savings of significant transport and dumping fees, the cost of 165,000 pounds of new steel, and the cost of 41,000 cubic feet of new concrete.

The interior architecture had to respond to 85,000 square feet of volume under a 20-foot-high roof structure. The library is patterned after a village; two primary corridors divide the space into "neighborhoods." Intersecting streets are differentiated; one is a vaulted, broad space topped with steel rafters and softly lit and the other is narrow and soars to a sky-lit roof that lets in copious light. At the intersection of the two main streets is the forum, which functions as a town square. Strong daylight reinforces the space's conceptual connection to traditional outdoor public spaces, while projecting a glowing beacon to the external community at night. This focal point is a place for welcoming the public, an area for social interchange, and a place for information and exhibition. The optimization of daylight reduces the facility's use of electricity and helps transform the previously characterless box into an inviting oasis.

Brightly colored landmarks, housing conference rooms and offices, are placed throughout the neighborhoods to help define street edges, gateways, and enclosure. The elements are placed to create maximum open area for future flexibility. The main landmark is the Information Services desk; in order to heighten its significance to the patron, the ceiling is cut out over this space in an oval shape, and suspended within is a wood and plate aluminum grid.

The glazed north wall creates a window to the street, displays the interior as a welcoming "people place," conveys the functions within the building, and functions as a lantern in the evenings. Color gels over soffit cove lights enliven the collections area and create an area of mystery at the public meeting room. The general collection and public meeting room flank the forum, central location the entrance with the parking lot. This playfully lit glass façade exudes the "soft high-tech" image of the library, which includes both advanced technological capabilities and an emphasis on person-to-person service. Shortly after it opened in 1995, the light-filled, technology-oriented facility was described by one patron as the city's own "Windows 95."

An arc of skylights rising out of the library helps give this former retail store a bold, civic presence. The front of the structure is primarily glass, bringing in copious light, exposing its function, and extending a welcoming gesture to the community.

FLOOR PLAN
1 – ENTRY PLAZA
2 – FORUM
3 – CIRCULATION
4 – INFORMATION
    SERVICES
5 – MICROFILM
    COLLECTION
6 – ONLINE SEARCH
7 – REFERENCE
8 – CONFERENCE ROOM
9 – AUDIO VISUAL CENTER
10 – PUBLIC MEETING ROOM
11 – YOUTH SERVICES
12 – PERIODICAL
    COLLECTION
13 – ADMINISTRATION
14 – RECEPTION
15 – TECHNICAL SERVICES
16 – TELEPHONE REFERENCE
17 – LOCAL HISTORY
18 – GENERAL COLLECTION
19 – COMMUNITY
20 – INFORMATION
    SUPPORT

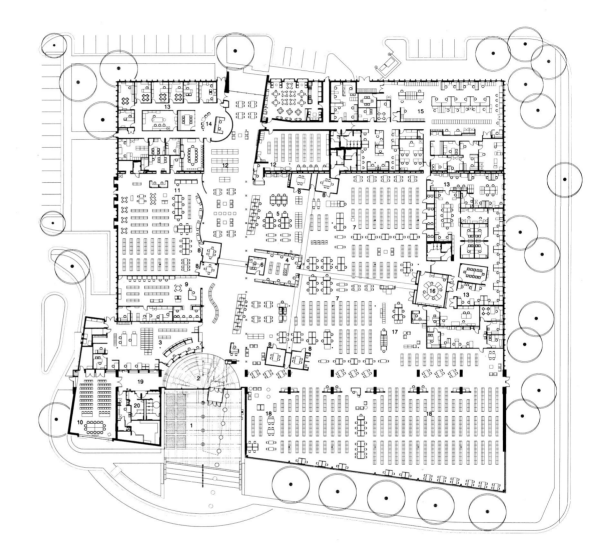

SECTION LOOKING NORTH

SECTION LOOKING EAST

Elevations, below, and sections, opposite bottom, show the long, low building that once housed a big-box retail use. After identifying an unconventional adaptive reuse as the cost-effective and environmentally sensible choice, the design team created an elegantly proportioned shape that rises from the flat roof. This element floods the interior with daylight and gives the structure a civic profile. Inside, the stacks, study and meeting areas, and research hubs are organized around two primary "streets" that create the town-like plan, opposite top.

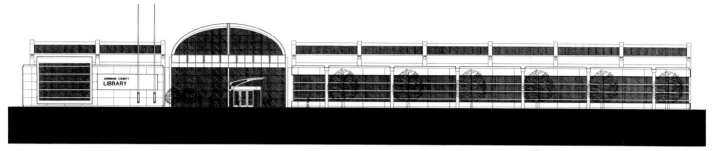

NORTH ELEVATION

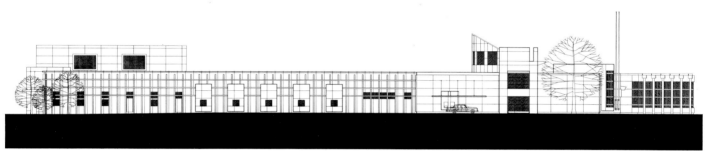

EAST ELEVATION

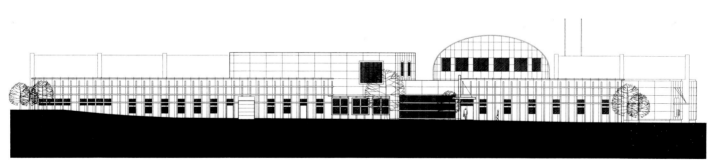

SOUTH ELEVATION

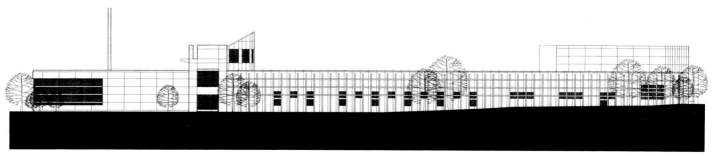

WEST ELEVATION

The elegant many-windowed structure (previous pages) no longer bears any resemblance to the bland box it once was. One patron dubbed the technology-oriented resource center "Windows 95." Steel beams and sweeping curves in the ceiling add visual interest and serve as wayfinding devices in the facility so that patrons can easily located the circulation area, right; study and meeting rooms, below; and the Information Services hub, opposite top.
Quiet study areas benefit from daylight, opposite bottom; low-e glass keeps heat gain down and the daylight helps minimize use of artificial light.

National Hurricane Center

Miami, Florida

This project is representative of the firm's long-term client relationships. After 10 years of working with the National Weather Service, the firm and the client embarked on this major project.

Located on the campus of Florida International University, with a collection of poured-in-place concrete structures, the site is adjacent to and clearly visible from a major highway. The visibility of this international icon was important to the client.

In response to Hurricane Andrew, national, state and local planners devised a stringent set of building codes for hurricane facilities that must withstand the direct effects of an "extreme" hurricane. This facility pioneered the first application of these new requirements. Two massive blocks of site-cast reinforced concrete with sand-blasted finish house support functions. They embrace the central "machine" that contains three operations rooms and supporting equipment. The north and south facades feature metal panels over the concrete structure and aluminum jalousie-shuttered windows.

The building is elevated five feet to free it from the storm surge plain, providing an additional layer of protection. Accomplished with external fill, the building's oversized spread footings, coupled with retaining curbs at the berm's edges, provide a stable base for the foundation and lend the facility a prominent profile.

To permit uninterrupted forecasting during tropical storms, all details were designed to withstand 130 mile-per-hour winds without damage. A variety of proven methods—including roll-down shutters, jalousie shutters, removable storm panels, and laminated glazing—were provided for all openings to supplement the 10-inch-thick concrete shell. A compact weather shelter, sized to accommodate staff and visiting media, is reinforced to withstand a direct hit by a 250-pound projectile at 60 miles per hour.

Creating an identifiable landmark that celebrates the National Hurricane Center's technology, the central spine links the facility's exterior equipment with the internal operations core. This provides an ordering system for the equipment and symbolizes the backbone of weather prediction. All exterior equipment is mounted to reinforced galvanized steel on the catwalk structure along the spine. The equipment layout on this catwalk prevents interference among the communication devices, the larger of which move continuously while tracking satellites.

The client's desire for visibility and height contrasted with the weather related need to protect the technology and personnel inside. Reinforced concrete with a sand-blasted finish proved part of the solution; an entry arcade is topped by the start of the structure's spine, below, which supports satellites and other elements of the facility's advanced weather-tracking technology.

SECTION

A – TECHNOLOGY/DATA
     BRIDGE
B – HVAC SYSTEMS
C – RESEARCH AND SUPPORT
     COMPUTER EQUIPMENT
D – TROPICAL PREDICTION
E – OPERATION
     NATIONAL HURRICANE
F – OPERATION
G – RESEARCH/SUPPORT
H – ADMINISTRATION

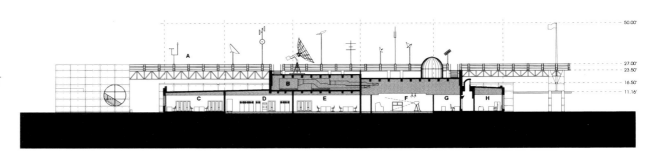

The facility, which was
already being planned when
new building codes were
being crafted, pioneered
the application of the new
requirements. This placed
limitations on some of the
interior spans and spaces.
Variety of materials helped
provide the solution;
a blend of brushed stainless
steel and exposed concrete
maintains visual interest
through a contradiction in
textures.

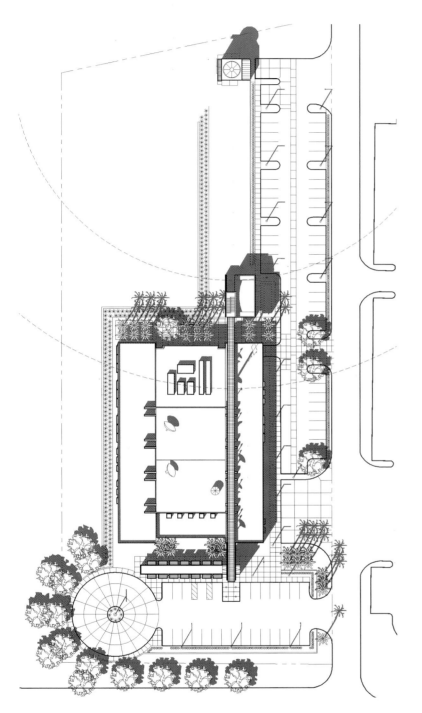

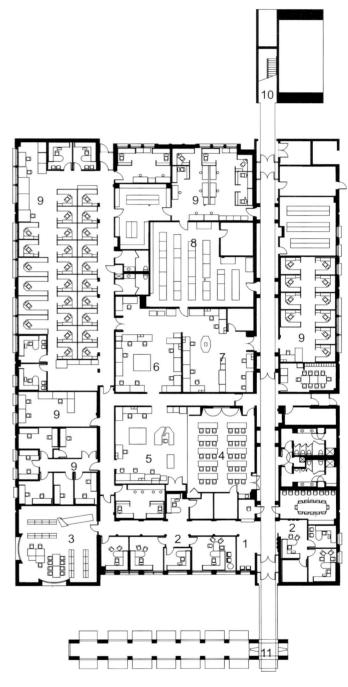

The site and floor plans, above, reveal how the form of the building was derived, in part, from the need for the structure to provide extraordinary protection during extreme weather. The most sensitive equipment and technology are located in the heart of the building, farthest from the fenestration at its periphery. The section, opposite top, shows the roof catwalk structure that runs the length of the building; this is where the exterior weather measurement devices are secured.

FLOOR PLAN

1 – LOBBY/RECEPTION
2 – ADMINISTRATION
3 – LIBRARY
4 – MEDIA/SEMINAR ROOM
5 – NATIONAL HURRICANE OPERATIONS
6 – TROPICAL PREDICTIONS OPERATIONS
7 – WEATHER FORECAST OPERATIONS
8 – COMPUTER EQUIPMENT
9 – RESEARCH AND SUPPORT
10 – ROOF CATWALK ACCESS
11 – COVERED ENTRY

A celebration of the National Weather Service technology is created with the central spine (previous pages) that links the exterior equipment with the internal "machine" of operations rooms.
A simple, efficient building form, opposite, was paramount to stay within tight budget constraints. Variations on form, texture, material and color differentiate working spaces, left, and reception, below.

Beth Torah Synagogue

Overland Park, Kansas

After master-planning, a new home was designed for this Reform congregation on a beautiful, rolling, wooded, 22-acre site at the confluence of two creeks in suburban Kansas City. Facilities serving this 450-family congregation include a sanctuary, administrative offices, classrooms, library, shop, and kitchen—all accessed by a large entry foyer that doubles as an interim social hall.

The site offers an enormous potential that is central to the facility's architecture. The creeks along the north and east edges of the site create a wide flood plain. The complex's design offers many views to the outside so the congregation can enjoy the site's beauty. The site gently slopes toward the creeks, providing areas for repose or small gatherings.

The design concept developed around several of the congregation's objectives, including the achievement of an intimate religious community of caring individuals; the embodiment of a modern Judaism expressing dedication to light, life, and unity; the idea of the synagogue as the province of all not the domain of the few; and the encouragement of participation where everything is touchable, even the sacred.

In response to the congregational mission and other imperatives, the building complex is an intimately scaled and unified cluster of building components—and abstract interpretation of an historic middle eastern village. Consistent with the congregational emphasis on community, an entry plaza and foyer give reference to a public square to enhance interaction. The foyer is conceived as a meeting place from which all the major building components emanate. It was designed with high ceilings, skylights, and clerestories that emulate the open feeling of the sky, thus bringing the exterior into this "public square."

The complex employs other examples of village patterning as well, such as landmarks, paths, and edges. The curving walls of the Transition, a wooden structure that houses the Heritage Torah, facilitates the transition from the public square/foyer to the sacred space of the sanctuary. At the approach to the Transition, the space becomes more narrow, the ceiling lower. Carpeting is introduced here, too; the goal is to quiet the mind on entry to the sacred space. Once inside, congregants face the Ark and the northeast wall of glass reveals a cluster of trees just beyond.

The sanctuary ceiling features circular disks that represent the community and its overlapping subsets. The lowered circular disk deflects sound toward the back of the sanctuary so that microphones can be avoided. Operable wall panels allow the expansion of the sanctuary for special celebrations. It was important to the synagogue leaders that the expansion seating not feel removed and that their sightlines and proximity to the Bimah (Torah reading area) be as intimate as possible for High Holy Day services. Fixed seating accommodates 375; 700 people can be seated when the expansion spaces are employed.

Simple forms and clean lines speak to the congregation's notion of a modern faith while the materials, scale, and arrangement of buildings in the complex refer to historic Middle Eastern villages and the long Jewish tradition.

The site plan shows the Beth Torah Congregation facility's orientation towards its wooded setting. The floor plan, below, shows the sanctuary's intimate layout, and way that the central plaza links the various components together. Dotted lines denote the planned expansion.

FLOOR PLAN

1 – ENTRY PLAZA
2 – VESTIBULE
3 – FOYER
4 – COATS
5 – SANCTUARY ENTRANCE
6 – SANCTUARY
7 – BIMAH
8 – EXPANSION MEETIN
9 – MEETING/CLASSROOMS
10 – LIBRARY/CHAPEL
11 – BRIDAL DRESSING OOM
12 – GIFT SHOP
13 – ADMINISTRATION
14 – RABBI
15 – SCHOOL DIRECTOR
16 – ADMINISTRATION
17 – WORKROOM
18 – STORAGE
19 – KITCHEN
20 – STORAGE
21 – BUILDING SERVICES
22 – SERVICE COURT
23 – ELECTRICAL
24 – MECHANICAL
25 – COMMONS
26 – MOVEABLE WALL
       STORAGE
27 – VENDING
28 – FUTURE PLAZA
29 – FUTURE SOCIAL HALL

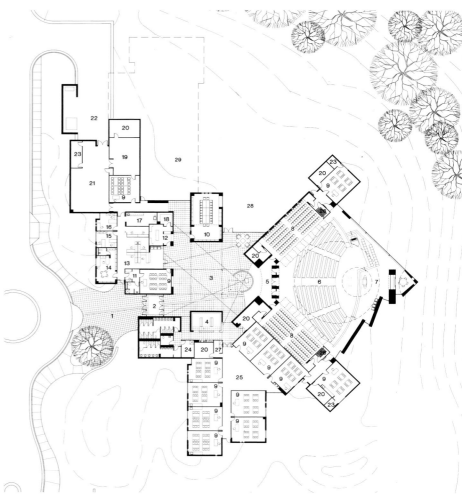

Simple, boxy forms nestle into the site. The smooth white exterior cladding pays homage to the architectural language of Jerusalem. The synagogue appears as a cluster of forms, no single form taking precedence, a physical representation of one of the congregation's missions—that the community, rather than the individual, is most important.

Pale exterior cladding (previous page) references the white stones used in Jerusalem. In the sanctuary, right and below, congregants look out onto the densely wooded site; an angled disk improves the acoustics for readings from the Bimah. The foyer, or public square, opposite, is the hub of the community. Its focus is the Transition, a semi-circular wooden structure that houses the Heritage Torah; seven steel columns symbolize creation.

Cathedral Social Hall

Kansas City, Missouri

A 15,000-square foot social hall addition and an outdoor courtyard have been added to this historic church in downtown Kansas City, Missouri. A consensus-building process produced a visionary yet realistic concept for the future of Grace and Holy Trinity Cathedral; this is the first phase of expansion. The sensitive addition is designed with limestone walls, clay tile roofing, and custom steel doors and windows to respect the Cathedral's historic nave and bell tower. The Gould Evans Affiliates design team worked with consulting architects Taylor MacDougall Burns Architects of Boston.

With the addition of Founders' Hall to the Grace and Holy Trinity Cathedral campus, the congregation affirms its religious mission, reaching outward to metropolitan Kansas City, the poor, its church, and its congregation. The work supports and expresses the liturgical intentions of the congregation in a building that creates continuity with the past and represents future goals.

Founders' Hall adds to the Grace and Holy Trinity Cathedral campus two interconnected spaces for social events—an indoor hall and an outdoor court. The court spatially unites the cathedral campus, creating an outdoor room for fair-weather events and a new landscaped entrance to the complex of buildings focused on the tower.

The new social hall accommodates community events in a vaulted 500-seat space in a variety of seating configurations or divided into meeting rooms.

The first floor includes ancillary foyer, coatrooms, kitchen, and restrooms. The lower floor accommodates the Kansas City Community Kitchen, which serves over 300 hot meals a day, as well as maintenance and storage rooms. The building integrates ministries to the underprivileged, to the congregation at large, and to community and even business groups: this fall it hosts a new "Music in the City" series, including public performances in both Founders' Hall and the cathedral.

Founders' Hall builds upon the formal order and character of the campus through the recombination of architectural elements, iconography, and materials.

The new gable roof, parallel to the existing Nave and Diocesan Center, composes a triad of related forms across the campus.

The roof pitches steeply over a central gathering space, akin to the nave. The north wall is a panoramic arc of windows to the lawn and trees, echoing the curve of the 1975 Diocesan Center and the window proportions of the 1895 Parish House, formally unifying disparate elements. Local limestone and red clay roof tile are used again, but express modern construction methods. The rubble of the new foundation walls recalls the old walls of the nave. The upper walls are made of precisely machines stones. Triangular prismatic columns of the new colonnade restate this quality in geometry that invokes the Cathedral's name.

The new roof lanterns symbolize the cathedral's renewed commitment to Kansas City. Crystalline forms, they relate in scale and shape to the city. Beacons signifying interaction, the roof lanterns are instruments of light exchange. By day the lanterns fill Founders' Hall with indirect light, conveying openness; the outward looking extroverted social space is a counterpoint to the dark, contained, and introspective nave. At night they communicate the *activity and activism* of the Cathedral.

Roof lanterns at the new social hall represent the Grace and Holy Trinity Cathedral's outreach mission and serve as nighttime beacons in the downtown Kansas City neighborhood.

FIRST FLOOR PLAN
1 – FLEXIBLE MEETING
    ROOMS
2 – SOCIAL HALL
3 – STORAGE
4 – COURTYARD
5 – GARDENS
6 – SANCTUARY

The social hall and courtyard
provide much needed space
to the congregation.
The footprint, form, and
materials of the new social
hall harmonize with the older
buildings on the campus but
resist imitation. The crisp lines
and machined stonework,
opposite, contrast with the
rubble stonework of the
foundation and elsewhere
on the campus. The lanterns
and windows in the social
hall provide copious natural
light in the primary
gathering space.

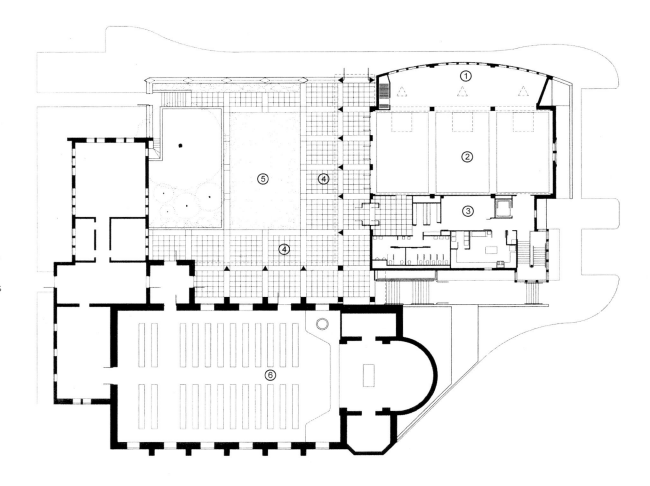

SECTION
1 – FLEXIBLE MEETING
    ROOMS
2 – SOCIAL HALL
3 – STORAGE

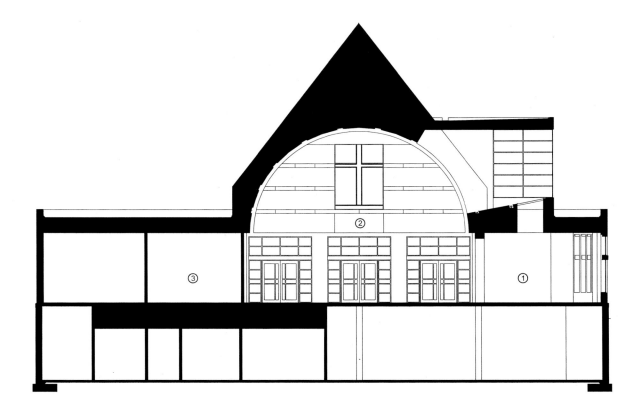

Westport Corporate Center
Kansas City, Missouri

To create a home for one of the firm's affiliates, the firm leaders looked to regenerating urban neighborhoods and then searched for adaptive reuse opportunities. The challenge was converting a cluster of defunct facilities into an innovative and technologically advanced offices space—and a really fun place to work. Utilizing existing structures made environmental sense and financial sense. The office was completed for approximately half the cost of a new building. The complex, which is located in the heart of a historic area, has also become part of the revitalization of the city's core. The 30,000-square-foot office is located in three adjacent structures: a brick and concrete industrial building with 15-foot ceilings; an abandoned retail mall with 40-foot ceilings and exposed trusses; and an office building with low ceilings. The design team had to find a way to unify these spaces and establish a new aesthetic for the buildings that would capture and project the dynamic nature of the design firm.

The design process was one of experimentation and collaboration and the projects is considered a work in progress. The creative resources of the firm were tapped throughout the project. The strong design concept worked toward a sense of coherence and integrity within the framework of a "warm industrial" aesthetic that combines the characteristics of a people-friendly environment with the expressive potential of low-cost, industrial materials. In addition to giving new life to a failed complex, the project reused materials, recycled demolition waste, and the specification of environmentally sustainable products where possible.

Entries into the office converge at the central piazza along an axis that begins at the street-front courtyard; here, an angled wall enters the building and it terminates at a freestanding lift enclosure adjacent to the scaffold reception desk. This wall is sheathed in patterns of perforated metal, revealing the structural steel and metal stud construction. Intersecting this axis is a 300-foot-long freestanding curved wall that arcs through the three buildings. Its profile undulates as it penetrates windows and new masonry openings. It stretches across the main stair, forming a gateway and defines the internal circulation path through the office. Behind it is a zone of special services (such as reprographics) as well as solitude nooks, and an art gallery. The wall was underpainted with vibrant color, topped with a muted tone, and raked, creating a colorful and textured surface.

The design team developed a new concept for an open office environment; it supports team-oriented work patterns and enhances project management and delivery. Variations on hotelling, virtual offices, and design phase-specific studios were explored. Ultimately, a decision was made to define teams by their centers, rather than their boundaries. Each project leader sits near an area of project resources known as a project center, which also serves as an informal meeting place and area of communication. Project centers shift and reconfigure often. The need for mobile furniture—everything is on wheels—was met by a diverse strategy of modifying existing furniture, custom designing some pieces, and working with Haworth's Crossings furniture to make it interface with the architecture. One custom piece, the reception desk, is hung from a four-tier mobile industrial scaffold. Screw jacks are used as finials, a plank outrigger supports computer monitors, and a power/data umbilical cord gives the unit flexibility—it can serve maintenance functions as well.

The adaptive reuse of parts of three buildings resulted in a vibrant, innovative office space with a strong sense of unity, and a sustainable, low-cost aesthetic throughout.

Site plans show the reuse
of three distinct buildings.
The center section was
the former retail space
and benefits from high
ceilings and copious daylight;
the other two utilize curves
to orient toward the center.
The section, opposite top, also
shows how the front
and back spaces are oriented
toward the primary central
space. The floor plans,
opposite bottom, show the
corridor in the center of the
project, the number of moves
that took place in each of the
three areas within the first
nine months of the facility
being opened, and the fluid
(anti-cube) furniture layout.

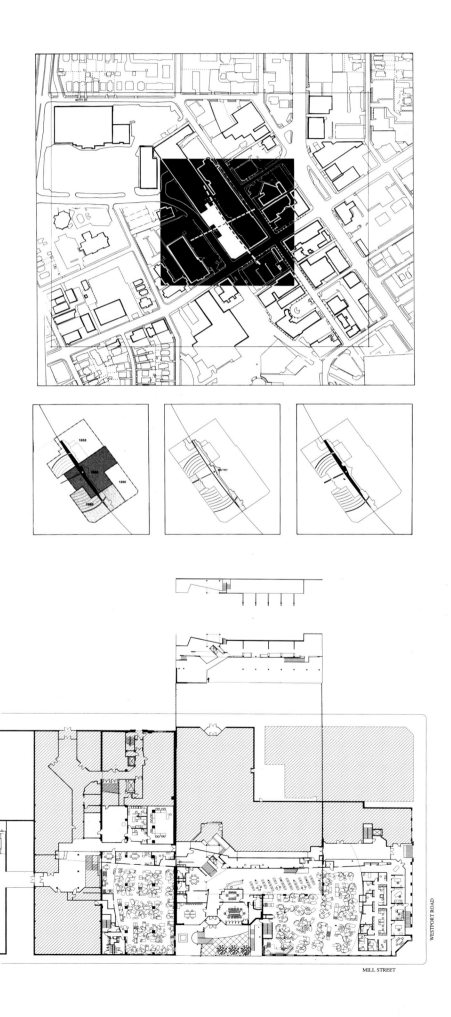

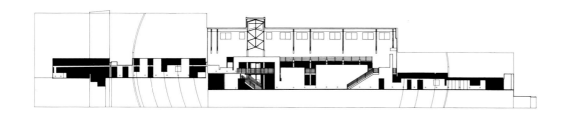

FLOOR PLAN
1 – ENTRY PLAZA/RECEPTION
2 – OPEN OFFICE
3 – PRIVATE OFFICE
4 – ADMINISTRATION/MARKETING
5 – MULTI-MEDIA CONFERENCE
6 – CHARRETTE
7– VENDING
8 – REPROGRAPHICS
9 – LIBRARY
10 – CONFERENCE
11 – TRAINING ROOM
12 – MODEL SHOP
13 – ENTRY COURT
14 – SOLITUDE NOOK
15 – PARKING

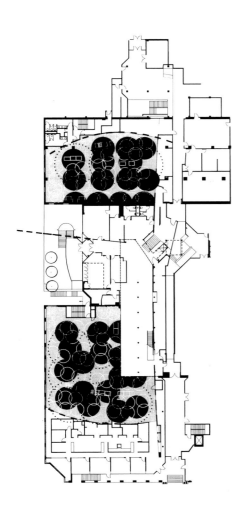

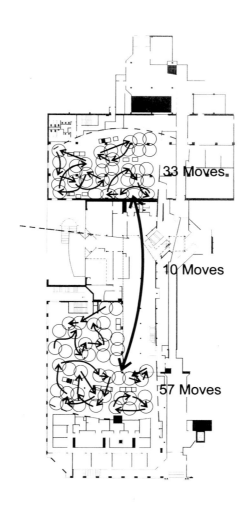

33 Moves.

10 Moves

57 Moves

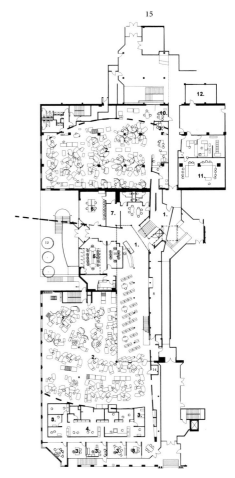

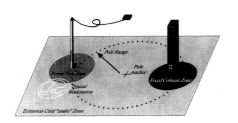

The two entries to the office converge at the piazza space and a dramatic reception station built from scaffolding, below. The metal stud wall begins out in the entry courtyard and penetrates the street-front façade, opposite.

Existing mezzanines in the center building were modified, extended and linked with bridges, ramps and stairs, right and below. A third-level loft was added beneath the clerestory, balancing on cantilevered beams.

W. Jack Sanders Justice Center
Overland Park, Kansas

The city leaders had several issues in mind when they began planning for this new police station and courthouse. Working with the design team from Gould Evans Affiliates, they identified four priorities. The facility must be designed to accommodate future expansion without disrupting existing functions. It must be open, user-friendly, and highly accessible. It must provide separate spaces for the police and court functions yet maintain a unified, civic presence. Finally, it must physically and functionally embrace security concerns. The facility gives the city a strong civic presence in a park-like setting, reflecting the city's openness and sense of community. The masterplan reroutes a proposed greenway to intersect with the building. Once the greenway is complete, the building will hold an important position along this green "thread" uniting the city.

The design permits maximum security through traditional separations. Juveniles are separated from adults in the holding cells and people being prosecuted are separated from the prosecutors and witnesses via multiple means of access to courtrooms and other spaces of interaction. A processing space and temporary holding area are located on the lower level. Courtrooms are designed for expansion as needed.

The departments are unified in the structure by its two-story arcade, the spine that runs the length of the building. This arcade provides access at numerous points and serves as the mechanism for simple, clear circulation. The arcade's east and west wall are asymmetrical, adding visual interest. Accent colors emphasize courtroom entries and public areas.

In order to create an uplifting environment outside of courtroom spaces, strong emphasis was placed on daylight, which pours in through the ceiling of the arcade. Thus, the common and circulation spaces require very little artificial lighting and they are airy, light, and pleasant, especially in contrast to the more cloistered courtrooms. The two-story arcade wall achieves a dramatic, civic scale without compromising the image of open government.

The new building's central arcade forms a spine and also creates the civic scale of the structure. A solid, masonry structure exudes the security that is related to its justice purpose, but the transparency of the top of the arcade helps to define this governmental building as one that serves and is open and accessible to the community.

The site plan indicates the planned expansion with shaded areas; the rear façade of the Justice Center was designed to interact with the additional structures. The section, below, shows how the facility utilized the grade change of the site, and how the central spine services both front and back. Floor plans, opposite, show how the detention spaces, courtrooms, and offices are kept separate, while the appearance and feel of the building is unified.

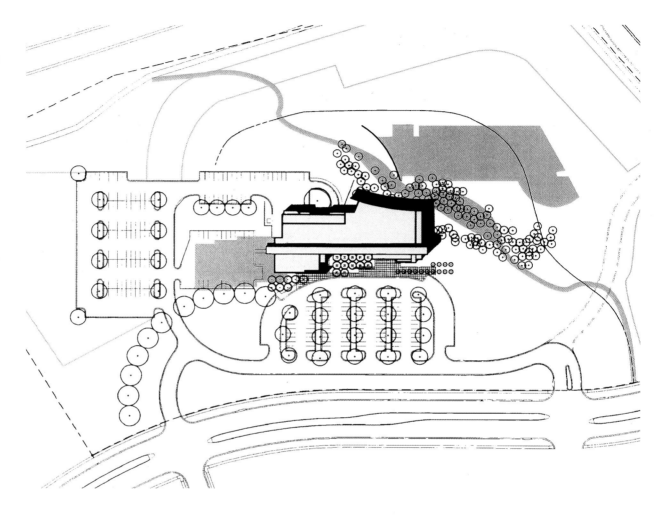

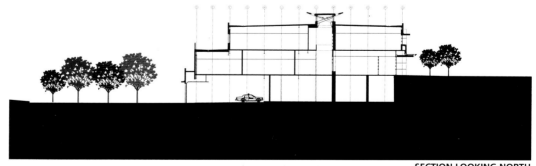

SECTION LOOKING NORTH

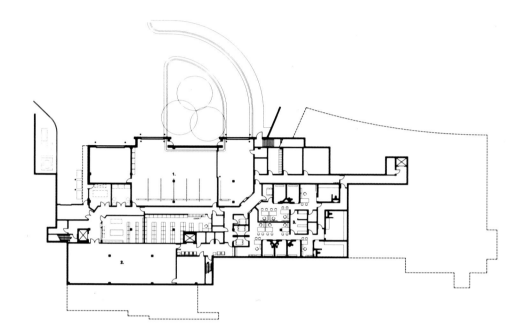

FIRST FLOOR PLAN
1 – SALLYPORT
2 – MECHANICAL
3 – BOOKING/DETENTION

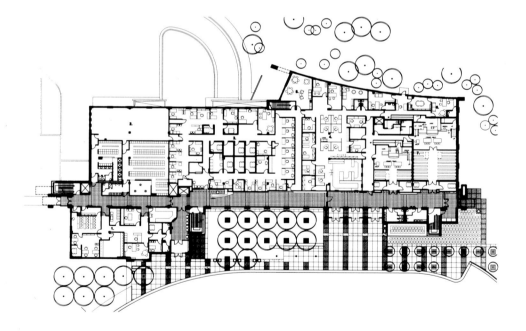

SECOND FLOOR PLAN
1 – POLICE OFFICES
2 – PHYSICAL FITNESS
3 – PATROL
4 – CLERKS
5 – BREAK ROOM
6 – JUDGE'S CHAMBERS
7 – COURTROOMS

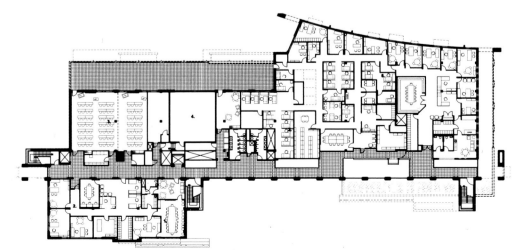

THIRD FLOOR PLAN
1 – CHIEF OF POLICE
2 – POLICE OFFICES
3 – TRAINING
4 – MECHANICAL
5 – PROSECUTORS

The lower level of the facility is devoted to the processing and detention functions, above, so that these are kept distinct from the offices, courts, and other upper-floor functions. The courtrooms are simple, elegant, and softly lit, right. The primary circulation space, the arcade that is the spine of the structure, opposite, is awash in daylight and offers views of the park-like setting; this space offers relief to the courtroom activities.

Community Health Facility

Lawrence, Kansas

The Community Health Facility integrates the services of four health agencies in one building. Although the Bert Nash Community Mental Health Center, the Lawrence-Douglas County Health Department, the Douglas County Visiting Nurses Association, and Hospice Care in Douglas County are funded differently and serve different members of the community, they are united in the goal of building a healthier community. The location of the new facility adjacent to the hospital places it as a new major contributor to the health care campus.

The facility brings together 85,000 square feet of office, classroom, clinic, exam, and public meeting space that addresses the agencies' desire for a contemporary but warm environment that is integrated into the rest of the health care campus. The building's profile complements the scale and character of the existing hospital and neighborhood.

The architectural detailing, such as the metal cornice, lends traditional detail and scale in contemporary methods and materials. The exterior material palette is a blend of the warmth and tradition of brick with the technology of metal. Glass corners greet the client, suggesting an open and accessible heath care environment. While a family of steel canopies establishes the architectural vocabulary for entry into the building, each entry is designed specifically for the population it serves.

The main entry turns toward visitors as they approach from the main access road. It is marked by a large "cap" and establishes an axial connection between agency entries on the left and the right. This gregarious entry and the public lobby that it leads to provide access to the agencies arranged in wings for natural daylighting. Although the staff entry on the opposite side of the building is created with similar materials and style, it is scaled back. Along the eastern side of the building are playful path and ramps that introduce the entry for special needs children. The canopy for this entry has a playful feel with its canvas "paper airplane" shape. A specific entry for special needs adults was designed with a garden and a private smoking area.

The interior palette utilizes wood-paneled walls at the public reception areas for warmth and color. Clerestory and shared lighting provide daylight to interior offices. In each agency's space, support services are placed in the middle of the wings with clinic, office, and classroom spaces arranged along the exterior walls for light. Public circulation patterns are reinforced with shaded tile on diagonals and ceilings designed with movement.

Client privacy and safety are key issues for each of the agencies. To restrict access to certain parts of the building, all of the public and heavily trafficked functions are accessible on the first floor.

Access to the agencies' office and exam areas are also controlled by strategically placed reception areas on each floor. Through its mixed use of modern and traditional materials as well as the balance of the unifying and the unique, the Community Health Facility offers a building where form truly follows function.

The new building capitalizes on the specific purposes of each agency by tailoring each space to facilitate quality health care. In doing so, the building design results in an efficient, safe and home-like environment for all who are served here.

The Community Health
Facility's main entry and street
presence speak to its public
nature; the design team and
client felt it was important
to convey a sense of openness
and accessibility, while still
attaining a civic scale.

In plan, the public and
circulation areas between the
two wings are clearly visible,
rotated off axis to create a
dramatic main entry and
volumetric interest.

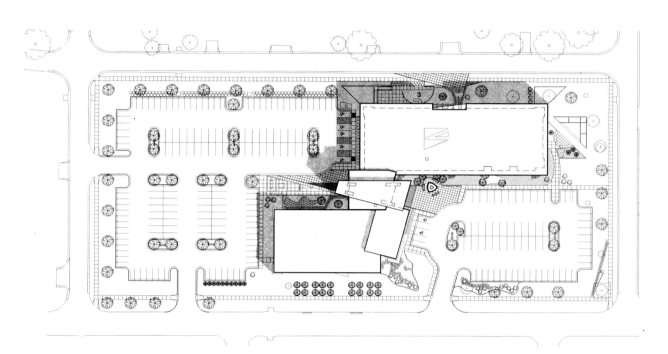

THIRD FLOOR PLAN

1 – CENTRAL LOBBY
2 – VISITING NURSES CENTER
3 – HOSPICE

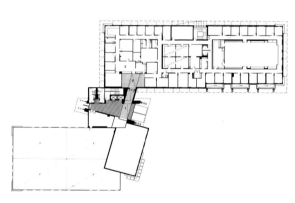

SECOND FLOOR PLAN

1 – CENTRAL LOBBY
2 – HEALTH DEPARTMENT
3 – BERT NASH CENTER
4 – COMMUNITY MEETING
   ROOM

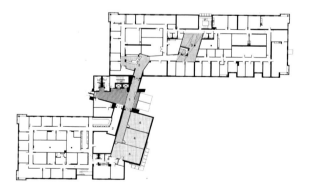

FIRST FLOOR PLAN

1 – MAIN ENTRY
2 – HEALTH DEPARTMENT
3 – BERT NASH CENTER
4 – MEETING ROOM

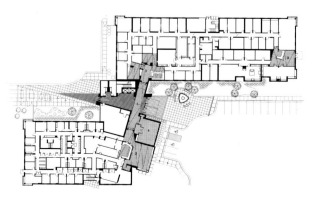

Glazing at the corner, left, is an expression of the openness that defines one of the public health agencies' shared goals. The rotated volume, below, accommodates the largest open spaces in the complex, the public health waiting area and the public meeting room.

Scale was important, and the
building's staff entry façade,
right, like the others, is a
civic presence. A large public
meeting room, below,
benefits from natural light.

Behind the scenes office space, left, is unusually diverse and benefits from varying ceiling heights and treatments as well as natural light unexpected deep within the building. Creative ceiling treatments, below, add interest in an antreach professionals' workroom.

Student Services Building

Phoenix, Arizona

The addition to and renovation of Paradise Valley Community College's Student Support Services Building responds to the center's new central position within the campus and its significance as a social and student service hub on the growing and evolving campus. It brings 38,000 square feet of student services into one building to provide one-stop access for students.

The design represents a collaborative team effort and the vision of the college, building committee, staff, and design team. The addition transforms an existing introverted mass into an outward reaching, indoor/outdoor environment. The entire south face of the existing building has been expanded.

A continuous steel canopy structure and landscape promenade organizes new building components alongside shaded outdoor space and spatially connects the existing campus to the west with the new and future growth to the east. This shade structure transcends the language of existing low horizontal canopies commonly used on campus into a grand public gesture.

One part of the facility, the student union, is a sun-protected, transparent box where student interaction is openly made visible to campus. By night, it continues to embrace the campus by transforming itself into a highly visible illuminated beacon.

The student leadership office is situated between the student union and the renovated dining area and announces its presence to the student body.

The material palette of new construction is a combination of masonry, glass, steel, and natural finish metals. It complements the color and scale of the existing building, while bringing a desirable new perspective to the campus. Zinc metal panels sheath a large angled wall, which itself acts as a backdrop for the union and as a visual terminus for the addition. Interior strategies included the removal of partitions to create an open environment. Upgraded lighting and light-colored wood finishes transformed the dark interior into a light-filled, welcoming space.

The Student Services Building presents a new profile toward campus. Transparency, allowing views into the building from outside as well as onto campus from within, was an important element.

FIRST FLOOR PLAN

1 – FINANCIAL AID
2 – FISCAL
3 – ADMISSIONS AND
      RECORDS
4 – SPECIAL SERVICES
5 – COUNSELING AND
      ADVISEMENT
6 – COLLEGE SAFETY
7 – GALLERY COMMONS
8 – STUDENT UNION
9 – STUDENT LEADERSHIP
10 – DINING
11 – LINE OF EXISTING
      BUILDING
12 – SHARED PEDESTRIAN
      ARCADE
13 – KITCHEN/SERVERY
14 – BOOKSTORE

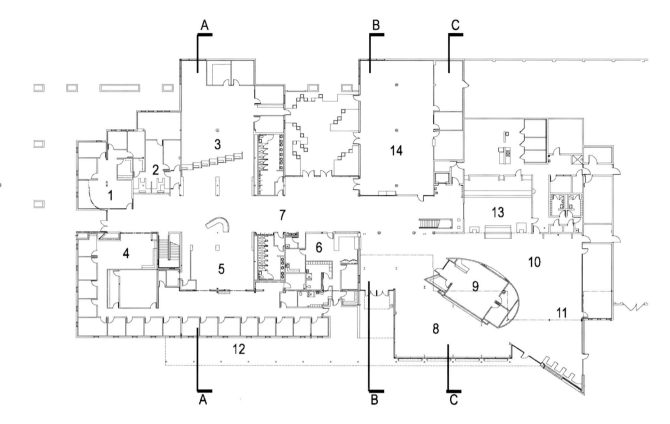

The site plan and floor plans
show the expanded Student
Support Services Building.
Outdoor spaces in this region
are critical, and here that is
articulated in the public-scale
arcade that shades the
student gathering spaces
inside and serves as a strong
visual marker of this facility.

SITE PLAN

1 – NEW STUDENT SUPPORT
      SERVICES
      ADDITION/RENOVATION
2 – CAMPUS PARKING
3 – PEDESTRIAN MALL
4 – EXISTING INSTRUCTIONAL
      BUILDINGS

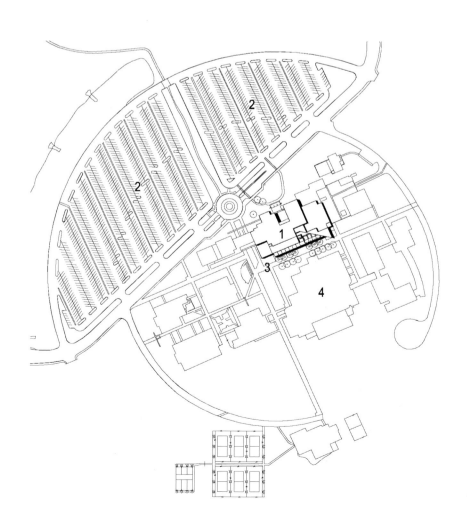

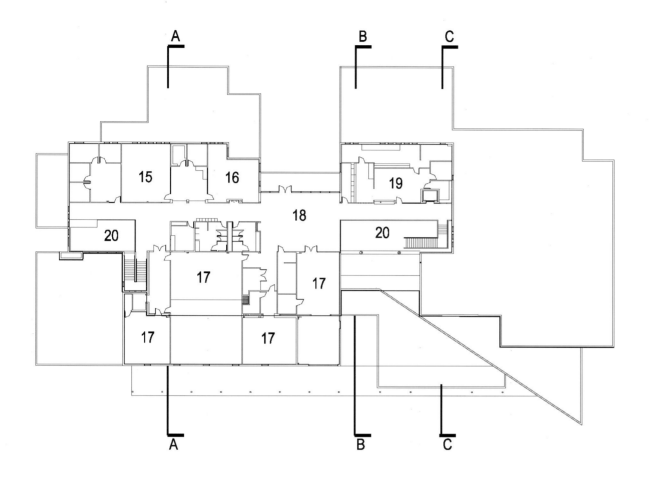

SECOND FLOOR PLAN
15 – ADMINISTRATIVE OFFICES
16 – TESTING
17 – CONFERENCE AREA
18 – GALLERY COMMONS
19 – IPC DEPARTMENT
20 – OPEN TO BELOW

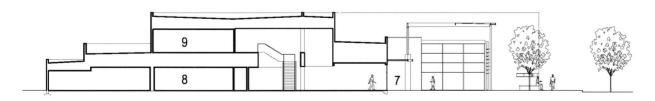

SECTIONS
1 – CONFERENCE
2 – GALLERY COMMONS
3 – COUNSELING/ADVISEMENT
4 – ADMISSIONS/RECORDS
5 – FACULTY OFFICE
6 – SHARED PEDESTRIAN
    ARCADE
7– ENTRY
8 – BOOKSTORE
9 – TESTING
10 – STUDENT UNION

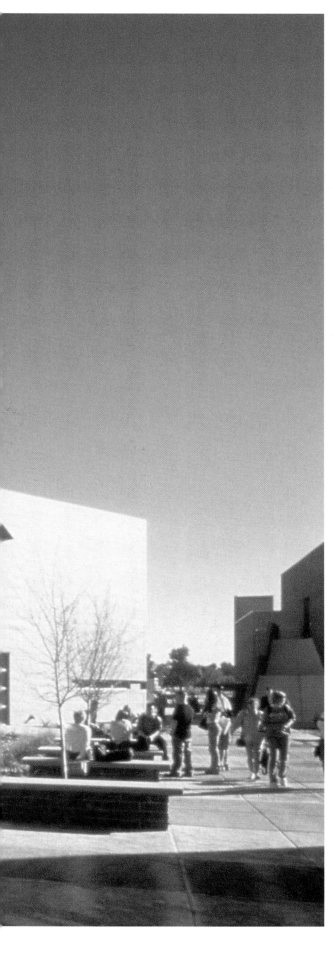

The glass volume, protected from the sun by shading devices and a canopy, extends the Student Support Services Building toward campus. Naturally finished zinc panel cladding creates a sleek skin that complements masonry and glass elements.
The new "glass box" is the center of student activity at the new facility. A canopy provides shade and creates a public-scale arcade that acts as an entry portal to the new building.

Outdoor spaces, opposite, are visually and physically connected to interior spaces, and intended to be furnished and utilized as an extension of the facility.

The student union gathering spaces, below, inside the new glass volume, are filled with light and afforded views, through the elegant louver system, to outdoor spaces and adjacent buildings on campus; this contributes to the important see-and-be seen social component of the facility. New dining space, left, and room for various groups to meet, were also part of the new addition.

Prairie Elementary School

Prairie Village, Kansas

The Prairie Elementary School in Prairie Village, Kansas, has been a long-standing institution for the oldest portion of Johnson County, originally opening in 1866. Then lightening struck it in 1990, destroying or severely damaging most of the building. Such was its importance to the community that neighborhood and alumni activism strongly urged a new building of similar character to be built on the same historic site. The programmatic requirements called for 63,000 square feet, comprising K-6 classrooms for 550 students, as well as a media center, music and art rooms, grade-level teacher's workrooms, gymnasium, and cafeteria with a proscenium stage, with relevant support spaces.

With the school's strong history, sentimentality among the neighborhood, alumni, and users set strong precedents to re-create a building that paid respect to the former school yet facilitated educational opportunities well into the next century. The existing neighborhood is a mature residential area in the older part of Prairie Village, an established Kansas City suburb. The site is bordered on the north and west edge by a well landscaped drainage canal, Tomahawk Creek, and across Mission Road is the Village Presbyterian Church, built in 1949.

The heavily trafficked intersection at 67th Street and Mission Road became a point of emphasis for the configuration of the new school's floor plan. The classrooms are oriented to the southeast, stepping back at the corner allowing a memorial courtyard to be visible from this significant intersection, and softening the impact of the institution upon the neighboring residences.

An existing entry portico and bay window were retained and restructured to serve as corner anchors for the courtyard. The edges of the depressed courtyard are defined by remnants of the foundation walls of the former school. Arising from the school's strong historical roots, the exterior is strongly driven by the traditional forms of its predecessor. Materials and colors were selected based on those salvaged from the original's remains.

Beyond the physical requirements of the program, the school district was interested in offering greater clarity between various grade levels, and encouraging more interactive teaching within common grade level classes. The interior focuses on the educational and emotional needs of the young students. The classrooms are organized into pods, or "neighborhoods," with colorful landmarks punctuating the center of each. Between classrooms, movable partitions are used to provide flexibility via larger shared spaces, allowing greater diversity of teaching methods. The perimeters of the classes are equipped with permanent computer workstations, allowing the center of the rooms to adapt to multitude teaching configurations. In each pod, two classrooms also share a small "reading nook," creating an intimate, light filled space in which small groups can engage in more individualized activities. From the exterior, these nooks provide a modern take on the bay windows of the original school.

The interior spaces are arranged with a two-story educational wing; a centralized administration area that opens into a two story lobby volume, and beyond, into an enclosed outdoor courtyard, harking back to the central court of the original school; and the larger ancillary spaces (cafeteria, kitchen, and gymnasium) to the west, away from the prominent intersection and adjacent to the play fields. The educational wing consists of classroom pods clustered around the central media library. Given the traditional importance of the library at the school, this space physically and symbolically occupies the most central and visible location, focusing toward the exterior and the Mission Road intersection, and opening on the interior to a dramatic two-story volume.

The exterior profile, massing, and materials were derived in part by the forms and hues of the original 1866 building, which had been almost completely destroyed by fire.

Many windows reinforce the connections between interior space and the site and a commodious entry courtyard allows for comfortable before- and after-school gathering and social activity.

The library, around which
the educational pods are
arranged, is a light-filled,
high-ceilinged space with
a wide range of study
spaces for individual
and small group work.

Corridors end in walls of glass, offering students, teachers, and administrators a strong connection to the grounds and flooding the halls with daylight. A sense of play pervades the interior spaces, opposite; varying materials and curved forms add distinction to the multiple spaces configured for many different styles of teaching and learning.

Language and Communication Building
Scottsdale, Arizona

The new Language and Communication Classroom Building at Scottsdale Community College brings together 28,000 square feet of classroom and lab facilities for the disciplines in the Language and Communication Division as well as for the Department of Communication and Performance Arts.

Through collaborative and conceptual planning workshops with the building committee, faculty, and staff, this new courtyard building establishes a unique campus precedent by integrating its internal classroom environment with flexible outdoor spaces.

The new design supports the vision of the campus master plan by sensitively preserving view corridors to the surrounding mountain context, reinforcing circulation patterns with shaded outdoor promenades, and providing an overall low building profile that complements the scale and character of the existing campus. The design of the building attempts to achieve strong dualities between building and site, mass and void, and light and shadow. Its form is expressed as a combination of masses whose varying heights signify their programmatic importance within the department and to the greater campus. The building is marked by a large entry portal, which establishes a strong axial connection to the existing campus and frames views to an internal courtyard beyond.

The courtyard is the perceived heart of the building. It serves as an informal gathering place to foster interaction between students and faculty and is the primary organizing space to bring together the various programmatic components of the building.

Carved into the earth and enriched with an indigenous landscape palette, a plaza and intimately scaled amphitheater provide additional outdoor teaching space. The monolithic presence of cast in place concrete walls reinforces the building's permanent relationship with its site. Native river rock and ground cover reference the cultural context and provide a textural setting.

The design efforts included the implementation of a new campus pedestrian mall. Indigenous shade trees, extensions of hardscape, and canopy structures all heighten the ambiguity of the spatial boundaries where building site ends and campus begins. The material palette of the building reinforces its relationship with the desert. The control and direction of natural light is expressed through the use of projected roof monitors, clerestory glazing, and sun protection devices. Perforated metal louvers work in tandem with the main horizontal canopy structure to shield the Writing Center from the sun, while preserving the view. Steel canopy structures define exterior circulation patterns and provide additional refuge and protection from the harsh desert sun. This new facility represents the collaborative efforts and manifests the energy of its users into a built reality that establishes a new identity and presence on campus.

The Language and Communication Classroom Building contributes to the overall quality of its campus environment and sustains the necessary enrichment opportunities for lifelong learning.

The building's entry portal establishes a strong axial connection to the campus and frames views to the internal courtyard. At dusk, the entry to the building, is softly but brightly lit and seems to glow from within.

1 – LANGUAGE &
    COMMUNICATION
    CLASSROOM BUILDING
2 – AMPHITHEATER
3 – EXISTING CAMPUS
    BUILDINGS
4 – PARKING
5 – AUTO DROP-OFF

The site plan, floor plans,
and sections show the
importance of the courtyard
as complementary teaching
and gathering space in the
Language and Communication
Classroom Building.

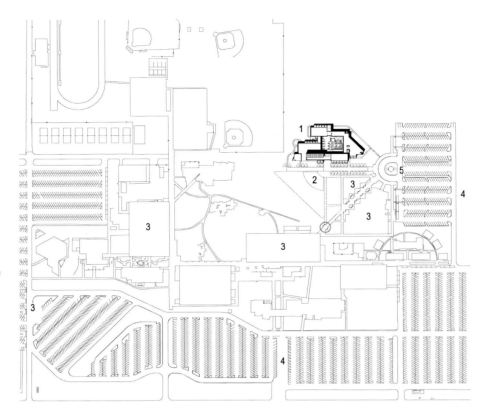

1 – EXTERIOR COURTYARD
2 – CLASSROOM
3 – SEMINAR ROOM
4 – TANDBERG LAB
5 – WRITING CENTER
6 – LECTURE HALL
7 – MOTION PICTURE STUDIO
8 – LOBBY
9 – CONFERENCE ROOM
10– FACULTY OFFICE
11– PEDESTRIAN MALL
12– STEPPED SEATING AREA

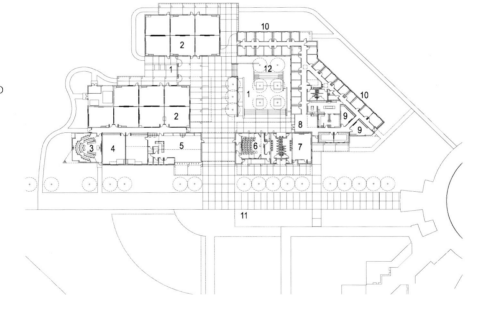

1 – ENTRY PORTAL
2 – EXTERIOR COURTYARD
3 – SHADED BREEZEWAY
4 – STEEL CANOPY
5 – LIGHT MONITOR
    CLERESTORY
6 – WRITING CENTER
7 – LOBBY RECEPTION
8 – CLASSROOM

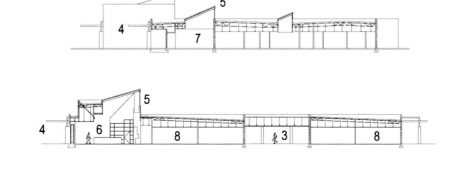

Overhead shade canopies filter
light, mitigating the harsh,
desert climate, while allowing
trasparency of the building
that accomodates views, a
connection with outdoor
spaces, and orientation
to nearby buildings and
the rest of the campus.

Interior reception spaces
facilitate a spatial and
material transition
from outside to inside.
Natural light and
connections to exterior
spaces and adjacent
buildings were important
considerations. A tiered
lecture hall, opposite top,
accommodates speech and
performance activities. The
writing center is naturally lit
through a continuous north-
facing clerestory element,
opposite bottom.

Museums at 18th and Vine

Kansas City, Missouri

An unusual urban development stands today as a testament to the will of the mayor, the tenacity of city officials, the creativity of the design team, the participation of the community, and the possibilities of a once-glorious neighborhood. Jazz and baseball stars made the Kansas City neighborhood around the intersection of 18th and Vine Streets famous decades ago.

From the 1920s to the 1950s, the neighborhood around Vine Street was abuzz nightly with jazz musicians playing at the Blue Room or the Subway Club, baseball players from the Negro Leagues, and hundreds of their fans. American jazz and sports history was made here. Connie Johnson, a star of the Negro Leagues' Kansas City Monarchs, recalls the area as "the Harlem of the Midwest—the place to be."After years of decline, the area now hosts a museum complex celebrating the African-American contributions to jazz, baseball, and the history of the city and the country. Two separate museums and a visitors center under one roof share a commodious entry space in the new structures, which manages to feel spacious inside while maintaining a pedestrian-friendly exterior presence. Like many mid-sized cities, especially those throughout the Midwest and the South, Kansas City has struggled to integrate disparate populations and fairly distribute resources throughout the community.

As a city councilman, Emanuel Cleaver II understood the divisions in the city, and hatched a plan to make a difference; he believed that healing some of the physical divisions could make a dramatic psychic impact on the citizens as well. His vision became known as "The Cleaver Plan," and he helped get the bond issue passed that would help fund regeneration in the neighborhood known as 18th and Vine.

The design team worked with the City and a redevelopment group to prepare a development plan for the nine-block area. The Gould Evans Affiliates team organized and scheduled the complex project and facilitated numerous workshops to achieve consensus among several cultural entities, community groups, political representatives, a marketing consultant, and design teams. Community participation was critical so that the community would feel a strong sense of ownership about the project once complete. Together, they worked to build on, rather than displace, the area's history.

The 85-year-old Gem Theater was restored, and across from it, a new, 55,000-square-foot museum complex was built. Street improvements included new trees, tree gates, sidewalks, and specialty light fixtures that recall the original character of the district. In one structure, the team had to weave together the needs of the baseball museum, the jazz museum, and the visitors' center—as well as making room for community uses that would vary widely. Early on, it became clear that some of the old structures could not be saved, so the team salvaged bricks and integrated them into the new structures. But the new facilities make no pretense; there was a clear mandate to avoid replication and strive instead for synergy of new and old. Completed in 1997 after years of planning, this cultural complex is proving to be a catalyst for broader renewal.

Use of brick was important
in order to pay homage to
the existing buildings,
but the design team also
wanted to create a building
whose contents would be
highly visible from the street.

So a stylized "arch"
became the gateway
to the new building.
Neon signage adds festivity
and a sense of the
entertainment focus
of this cultural complex.

KEYSSITE PLAN

1 – JAZZ MUSEUM
2 – 18TH AND VINE THEATER
3 – LOBBY
4 – NEGRO LEAGUES
      BASEBALL MUSEUM
5 – EXHIBIT HALL
6 – PLAZA
7 – GEM THEATER
8–   PARKING

The site plan, right, shows
how the project relates to the
neighborhood and orients
particularly to the Gem
Theater across the street.
The off-axis orientation
of the new museums
complex, below, helps
establish the structure as
contemporary.
The rear façade, opposite top,
was designed with musical
references in its cladding. The
street façade, opposite center,
corresponds directly to the
scale of existing structures in
the neighborhood, and utilizes
lots of glass so that activity on
the street can be seen from
within the museum lobby.
The section shows how the
lobby is shared by the jazz
museum, to the left, and the
baseball museum, to the right.

THEATER FLOOR PLAN

1 – JAZZ MUSEUM
2 – 18TH AND VINE THEATER
3 – LOBBY
4 – NEGRO LEAGUES
      BASEBALL MUSEUM
5 – EXHIBIT HALL

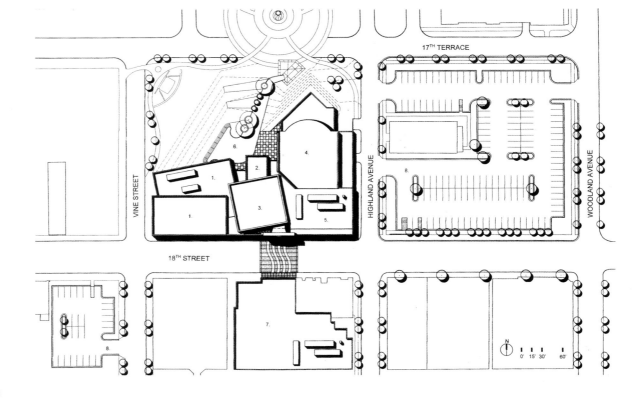

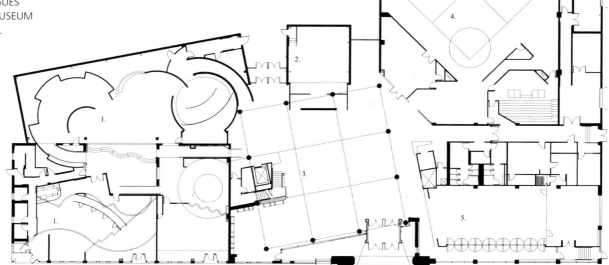

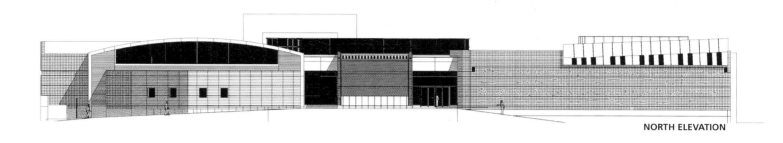

NORTH ELEVATION

SOUTH ELEVATION

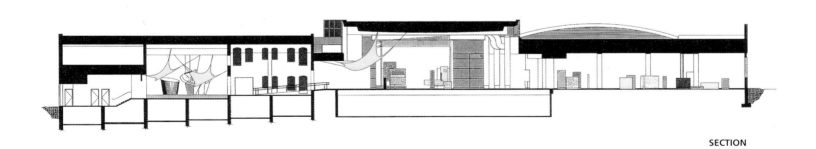

SECTION

The back of the new museums building opens onto an outdoor performance space. The design team elected to forgo historicism, preferring a synergy between old and new to an imitation. A keyboard and musical notes are abstracted into the façade.

The glass façade ensures that the community and cultural events held inside the museums complex are not isolated from the activity on the street. This was an important goal of the project, due to the long and vibrant history of the neighborhood.

The spacious lobby of the museums building, above, allows community gatherings of all sizes. Façade windows bring in light and make the space feel a part of the streetscape. The jazz museum's interactive exhibits, opposite top, are built around a collection of musical artifacts. Colorful fabric in asymmetrical shapes adds festivity to the jazz museum entry, opposite bottom right. The building also includes gallery space for local artists and students as well as office space in the mezzanine, opposite bottom left.

Unitog Corporate Headquarters
Kansas City, Missouri

The Unitog Company desired an 80,000 square-foot corporate headquarters that would be responsive to the area's diverse, historic context, a prominent downtown corner site that serves as a gateway into the urban core. To maximize the floor plate and minimize the apparent mass, the building is L-shaped. Entry points occur at the center, one from the parking court, and one from the "urban core."

The combination of materials responds to the aesthetic voices in its setting. Brick nods to the warehouse buildings in the area and warm-tone pre-cast concrete references adjacent stone cathedral. The metal panel and sunscreen cornice speak of contemporary technology with classical parti of base, middle, top. The curtain wall expresses lightness and transparency. Bricks are smooth cut on façades and rough cut at the corners; this articulates the corners effectively, and still renders the sleek, contemporary overall appearance. Glazed terra cotta and spandrel panels of complementary brick colors with relief provide interest. Below-grade parking allowed the designers to deal with the site's grade changes and create a plinth for the building.

The building's elliptical lobby and naturally lit grand space give this large facility an unexpected intimacy. The lobby's focal point is its glass bridge, which connects offices on the third floor. The lobby receives copious daylight, thanks to sculptural slices in the lobby ceiling. The design rotated the lobby 45 degrees while leaving the bridge on the orthogonal, creating a dynamic spatial rotation.

On a highly visible downtown site, the corporation's home was designed to be both referential to its context and contemporary in its form and materiality.

SITE/FLOOR PLAN
1 – BUILDING LOBBY
2 – AUTO COURT
3 – OFFICE
4 – SERVICE

The L-shaped building, as the plan shows, features two entry plazas that converge on an elliptical lobby. This dramatic space is also visible in the section, which shows how the floors of offices benefit from the light and air provided by this atrium space.
Variation in materials provides interest on the façades, opposite.

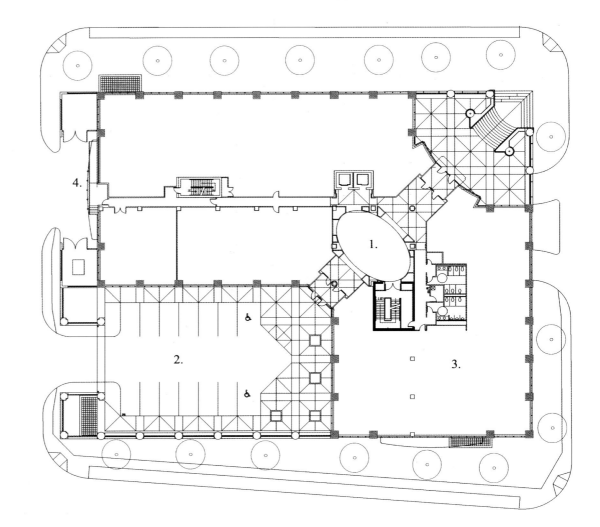

NORTH/SOUTH SECTION
1 – BUILDING LOBBY
2 – AUTO COURT/MAIN
      ENTRY
3 – OFFICE
4 – UNITOG
      RECEPTION/LOBBY

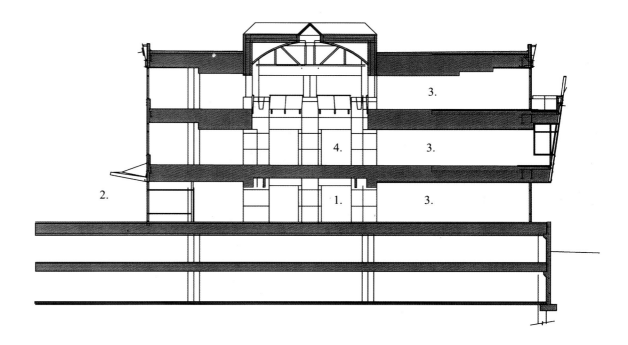

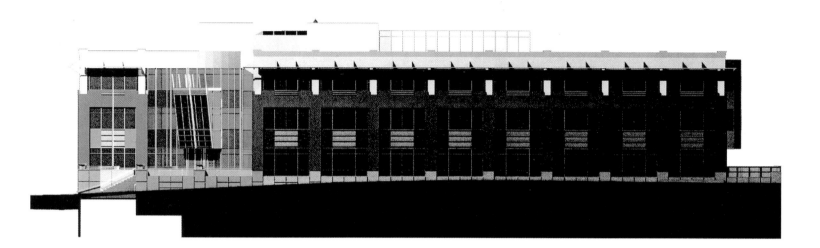

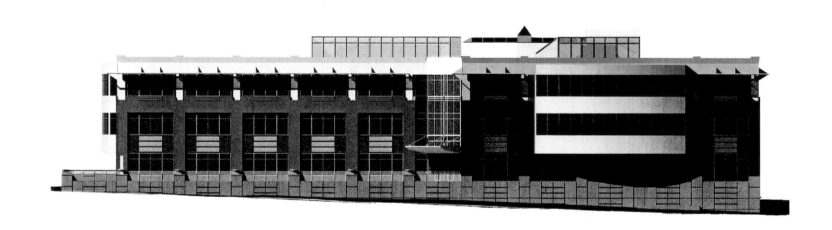

An eclectic mix of materials on the building's skin, opposite and above, make this a building very much of its own time and place but also at home in a downtown with many historic structures. The use of brick references the warehouse buildings in the area.

The centerpiece of the structure is the dramatic elliptical lobby, below, and its glass bridge, left, which connects offices on the second floor. This space receives a great deal of daylight, thanks to the highly sculptural "slice" in the lobby's ceiling, opposite.

State of Kansas

The State of Kansas work by Gould Evans Affiliates represents the kind of long-term client relationship that has helped build the firm in the last 25 years. Listed and shown here are a few representative projects.

The 1979 renovation of Marvin Hall for the University of Kansas School of Architecture and Urban Design demanded reconfiguration of spaces and new finishes for 30 faculty offices, 20 design studios, eight studio support areas, a resource library, a slide library, a jury room, a shop, and administrative offices. The resource library is located on the upper floor of the 1909 building to take advantage of the aesthetic quality of the timber roof trusses and skylights. Daylight was critical in this space and it remains one of the most pleasant and highly used areas of the building.

At the William Allen White School of Journalism and Mass Communications at the University of Kansas, a major renovation reorganized circulation, redefined common spaces, and updated offices and classrooms. The project also included a new, wired library and redesigned newsroom within the historic limestone structure.

At the Overman Student Center at Pittsburg State University, the challenge was to infuse the heavily used, worn building with new function and new life, and add a welcoming new entry. The design re-creates the building, giving it a bold profile and a strong sense of place, by striking a diagonal line through the public and retail spaces, linking the existing and new entries and defining circulation paths and lounge spaces.

The firm completed a renovation of the Memorial Student Union at the University of Kansas, the facility that serves as the campus "living room." The design team recognized the character of this oft-updated facility, and worked to streamline its image without losing the idiosyncracies that have become part of its campus profile. The firm has recently been commissioned to execute the next, more dramatic, phase of renovation.

Plumb Hall houses the central administration functions of Emporia State University. This small college town's main street terminates at Plumb Hall, which serves the gateway between town and campus. The renovation included the reconfiguration of offices, classrooms, an auditorium, and computer facilities, and the redesign of the entry plaza.

Transforming the aging Snow Hall complex into a state-of-the-art home for the University of Kansas School of Mathematics and Computer Science involved creating a framework for classrooms and offices and adding meeting spaces and a library. Raceways allow maximum flexibility in technology accommodation. The design team transformed a narrow link between two buildings into a special, skylit space.

Also at the University of Kansas, the firm is working on a major addition to the School of Engineering, and completing the transformation of a former residence hall into the School of Education. A significant addition to and renovation of Pearson Hall provides the school with flexible spaces that encourage teaming. The building's appearance is being completely redefined; elegantly articulated fenestration and brick detailing help give it a contemporary face.

Overman Student Center
Pittsburg, Kansas

The reconceived and expanded Overman Student Center has regained a visually prominent place on the campus at the University. As visitors, students, instructors and staff turn on the one way entrance road to campus, they now see a glass entry beacon presenting a union that is open, inviting, accessible and renewed.

School of Education

Lawrence, Kansas

The addition of the Teacher Education Center, off axis to the main building and incorporating a large partially cylindrical element, adds a dramatic entry and provides the School of Education with a distinctive campus profile.

Memorial Student Union

Lawrence, Kansas

A formal entry portal was created to allow a more ceremonial entry into the building; a large plaza offers gathering space. Inside, there was little continuity. Some square footage was added judiciously to clarify interior spaces.

The renovation also included adding banking and postal facilities, new restrooms, and information and retail booths on the main floor.

A special feature of is the gallery and exhibit space, which allows for the convenient change of exhibits and includes a highly flexible lighting design. The firm also provided easily interpreted signage that incorporates a silhouette of the facility.

Administration Building
Emporia, Kansas

The extensive renovation of Plumb Hall included the restoration of several significant historic features of the building. The entry was updated to gain a contemporary profile in the context and materials of its historic fabric. Signage and wayfinding solutions were integrated into the interior renovations to make this building accessible and comfortable.

School of Mathematics and Computer Science
Lawrence, Kansas

The exterior of the original Snow Hall building retains its original appearance. Inside, spaces are fresh and contemporary, while respectful of the building history. One of the most contentious of the existing conditions was a narrow connection between two of the buildings. The design team turned this into an opportunity for a commodious corridor topped with skylights, which has become one of signature spaces in the new facility.

School of Journalism
Lawrence, Kansas

Flint Hall occupies a prominent location on the University of Kansas campus, and is home to the William Allen White School of Journalism and Mass Communications. The historic limestone structure's arched openings provide views from and into the relocated and updated newsroom of the award-winning campus newspaper. A commodious reading room offers a variety of study spaces and access to the school's extensive resources.

School of Architecture
Lawrence, Kansas

When the project began in 1979, Marvin Hall was the oldest unrenovated building on the University of Kansas campus. Several arched openings that had been closed were reopened and numerous arched corridor windows were taken to the floor to open the corridor to activities and light.

American Multi-Cinema Theatres

The American Multi-Cinema Theatres projects that the firm has worked on in recent years represent an important part of the firm's story. The firm has had the opportunity to participate in the conception, planning, design, and detailing of theaters around the country, as well as in Canada, South America, Europe, and beyond. The design teams have been working at the leading edge of theater design and the wide range of urban, suburban, and technological issues that accompany this area.

Another important facet of the relationship with this particular client has been the opportunities it has presented for the Gould Evans Affiliates teams to work with other firms—architects, interior designers, and many others—on projects all over the world. This kind of collaboration has been a part of the Gould Evans ethic since the firm's inception. In many AMC projects, the firm works with other designers; for instance, the firm has collaborated with Ben Thompson Associates on New York's 42nd Street Empire Theater.

But the real rewards relate to the building type itself. Often these projects are not just theaters but actual entertainment destinations, whether they are urban (such as The Forum, in Montreal) or suburban (such as Westminster Promenade, near Denver).

The opportunity to work on the complex, synergistic relationships between retail, entertainment venues, restaurants, and other businesses has been a rich one for the firm, and the results have been rewarding.

Westminster Promenade
Westminster, Colorado

The theater, the largest in Colorado with 24 screens and 5,008 seats, is set in Westminster Promenade, a pedestrian-oriented entertainment, retail and office center, which will contain about 130,000-square-feet of retail specialty shops and restaurants and an ice skating center with three rinks. The Colorado sandstone edifice looks out over a paver courtyard and promenade lined with benches, planters, a children's play structure and a pop jet fountain. The walkway will lead to the ice rinks, two low-rise office buildings, a 350-bed Westin hotel and conference center and a botanical garden. The Promenade design, anchored by the AMC Theatre, forms a new hub for the City of Westminster, Colorado.

The theater offers the company's specialized seating with plush, high-backed seats with double-wide, cushioned and retractable cup-holder armrests that lift up. Each auditorium features stadium seating, allowing for optimum sightlines. Seat rows are 46 inches apart (six inches greater than the industry standard), allowing increased legroom and accessibility. An 18-inch rise between rows virtually guarantees unobstructed viewing.

Westminster Promenade is the product of a synergistic process involving city leaders, designers, developers, and leasing agents. Originally proposed as a project that included a theatre with retail pad sites, city officials saw an opportunity to create a neighborhood of cultural and recreational attractions that would become a community focal point. The City of Westminster honored Westminster Promenade with the 1998 Award for Excellence in Design and Development.

The sandstone façade opens onto a large plaza with detailed paving, fountains, benches, and other features designed to encourage outdoor gathering. The Colorado setting provided inspiration for the abstract tree motif. Special lighting and signage as well as intricate detail work inside and add contribute to the air of festivity.

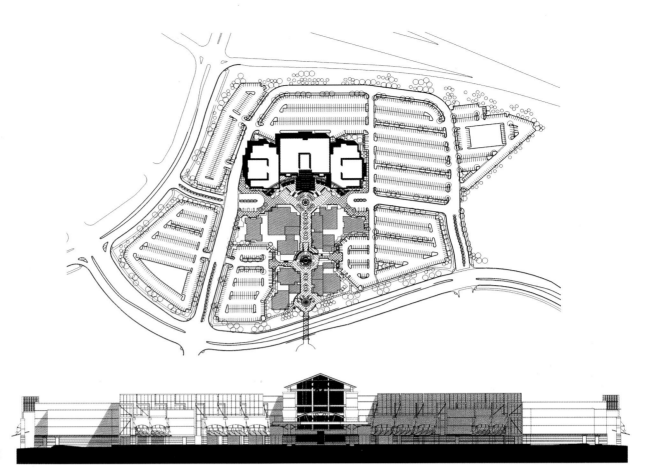

The site plan and elevation, right, show how the façade of the theater complex hugs the expansive plaza, which narrows to a promenade that fronts a series of retail and entertainment uses. The floor plan, opposite, is a symmetrical arrangement of 24 theaters; the four largest are in the center with the largest concession area adjacent. The section shows the use of tree-like interior ornament, playing on the Colorado setting.
Spacious and accessible concession areas are well lit and designated by a whimsical wave motif, right, and dramatic lighting, opposite.

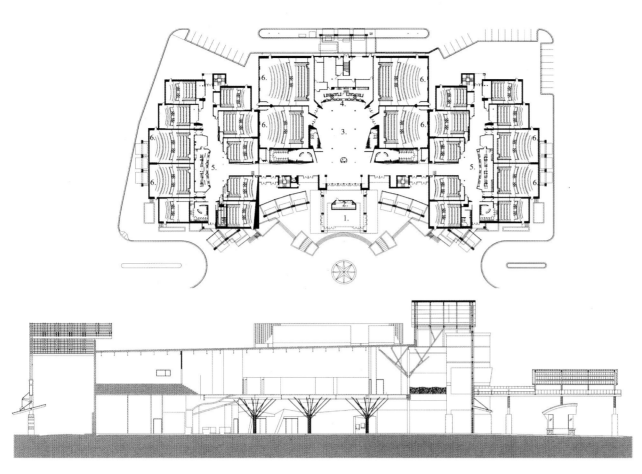

FLOOR PLAN

1 – VESTIBULE
2 – TICKET BOOTH
3 – MAIN LOBBY
4 – MAIN CONCESSION
    STAND
5 – SATELLITE CONCESSION
    STAND
6 – THEATERS (24)

Pleasure Island
Lake Buena Vista, Florida

The organization of the theaters and other spaces is designed with fluid circulation firmly in mind; this open, dual-level approach also allows for the see-and-be-seen atmosphere that helps imbue entertainment venues with a sense of excitement and communal experience. Each auditorium in the facility is designed to showcase the state-of-the-art sound and projection technology and is flexible enough to adapt to the next generation of that equipment.

A 65,000-square-foot addition to American Multi-Cinema's Pleasure Island location brings the complex to 24 screens and 110,000 square feet. A new focal entry was created to be responsive the new entertainment district being developed on the site by the Disney Corporation. Dramatic, large cylindrical forms create the entry portal, and neon and other lit signage broadcasts a vibrant invitation to those in the vicinity.

The client and the design teams worked hard to ensure that the large-scale façade would be countered by carefully designed elements at the human scale; it was important to keep in mind the pedestrian nature of the district. Two of the new auditoriums incorporate more than 600 seats with multiple balconies. This structure provides all auditoriums with the latest sound and projection technology, and is designed to accommodate further technological developments.

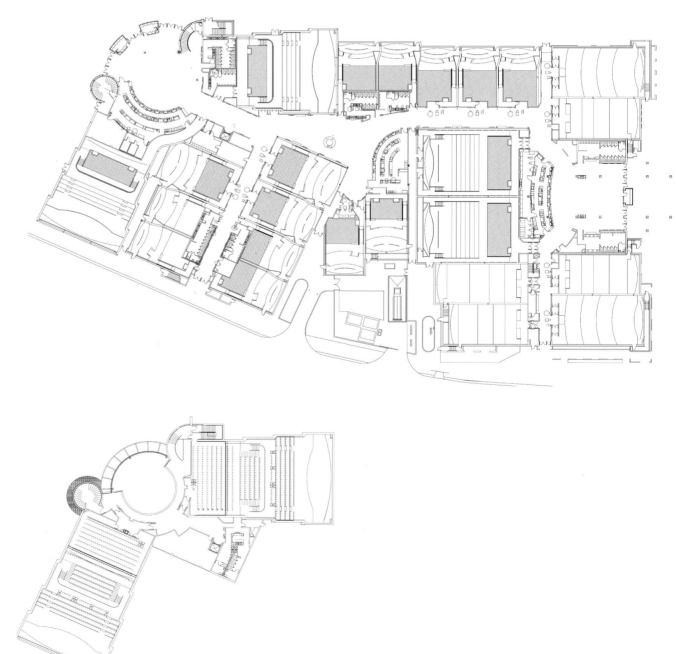

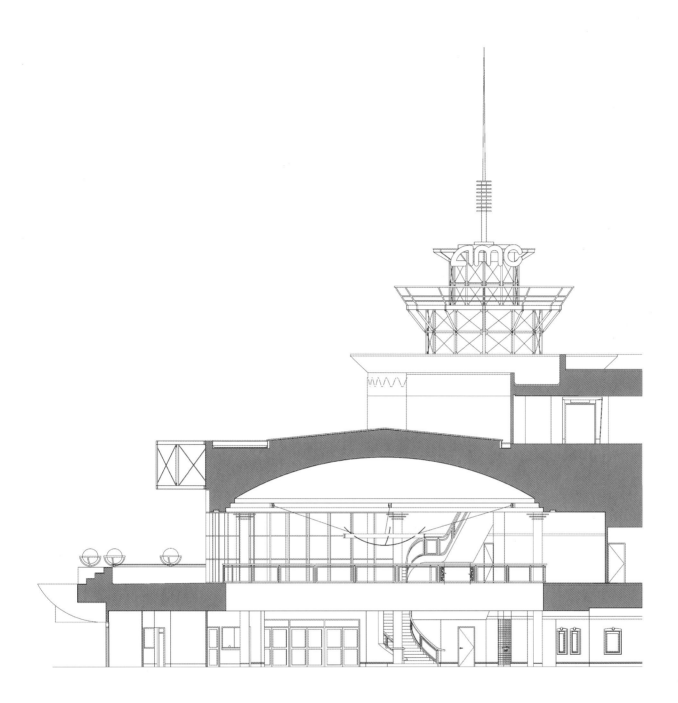

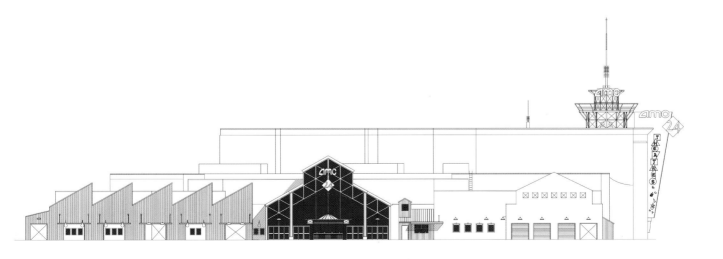

The multiplex at Pleasure Island, part of a new Disney entertainment district, is designed to create a festival atmosphere alive with light. The building's cylindrical forms frame the entry, and neon and other lit signage broadcasts a vibrant invitation.

Highly visible and accessible concession areas were a priority at this theater. Another important component was to make this grand-scale space seem comfortable at the human scale; this was accomplished through attention to detail and signage.

42nd Street Empire Theater
New York, New York

The AMC Empire 25 Theatres complex—part of Times Square's dramatic transformation—opened recently on 42nd Street. The historic Empire Theater was transported 170 feet down its block in preparation for the conversion. A large multidisciplinary team, including Gould Evans Affiliates, designed the major entertainment and retail development that includes a 25-screen theater.

This is among the largest and tallest multiplex ever built. The theater is more than 185,000 square feet, towering 176 feet above the street on 13 levels made up of six floors, two balconies, and five mezzanines, more than perhaps any movie theater in the world. The 93-year-old Empire Theater, one of seven Landmark-status theaters on that block, serves as the main entrance and lobby for the new complex.

The project required careful coordination with the New York City Landmarks Preservation Commission. The plan for the Empire reflects the complexities involved in large-scale renewal on a block in which a city's history has so many landmark restrictions and a determination by the developers to blend the architectural treasures of the past with the present.

The design team also worked with signage guidelines established for the Times Square area, and crafted a dynamic and vibrant façade in response.

The historic Empire Theater façade provides the main entrance to the movie theaters at the 42nd Street Empire Theater complex, which will be linked to a hotel, restaurants, and shopping areas. The façade of the rest of the complex is, in true Times Square style, a riot of high-technology, heavily lit signage.

Arrabida
Porto, Portugal

The firm's involvement with Arrabida, a 20-screen multiplex just outside Porto, Portugal's city center, meant collaboration with a large and diverse team. Gould Evans Affiliates was brought in to deploy its expertise and experience with the myriad issues that make American Multi-Cinema theaters function so effectively.

This included everything from the shape and layout of the auditorium, the design and technological considerations of the projection booths, and the important details relating to the expansive concession areas. Working with a Lisbon-based firm, the Gould Evans Affiliates teams worked to create optimal auditoriums with better-than-industry-standard sightlines and screen sizes. Other issues included the complicated relationships between the auditorium entry ramps and sloped seating as well as side wall splays (critical to optimization of acoustics), specialized seating and installation, and appropriate finishes.

The 92,000-square-foot multiplex, which is located in a shopping mall development just across the river from Porto's city center, is very large for this part of Europe, and within one year of its opening, it became one of the company's best-selling theaters. Part of a newly developing area of the city, the mall has proved successful as well.

The Forum
Montreal, Quebec, Canada

Built in 1924, a large brick arena was built in Montreal for the city's hockey team. In the 1960s, this was expanded and modernized. The Beatles played there and it was also the site of Nadia Comaneci's historic "perfect 10" during the 1976 Olympics.

The arena has long been considered the primary entertainment venue for the city. Now, this popular destination is being recycled yet again; soon it will house a three-level multiplex of 22 screens and 4,300 seats; the theaters account for more than 100,000 square feet.

In addition, theme restaurants, interactive gaming, and retail will grouped around a central interior plaza space that will be used for special events and will pay homage to the original "center ice."

New Work

Renaissance Hotel and Convention Center
Richardson, Texas

As a part of the Galatyn Park Development in Richardson, Texas, developer John Q. Hammons is creating the Renaissance Hotel and Convention Center. This will be part of a mixed use master plan that also includes a performing arts center, pedestrian plaza, high speed trasportation link, and a office complex that includes the regional headquarters of several corporations. The 335-room hotel will be 13 stories; a pedestrian plaza will provide an important link between the offices, conference center/hotel, and performing arts center. The design team has worked with other designers to achieve a contextual, holistic appearance in the complex; the goal is to speak the same language (a sleek, high-tech aesthetic) while maintaining individuality and distinction and at the same time, push the boundaries of what can be created on this site.

The designers are also exploring the possibilities of using greywater recycling systems (or comparable technologies) due to the fact that aquifier stability in the region is a pressing issue, especially for laundry-heavy hospitality businesses.

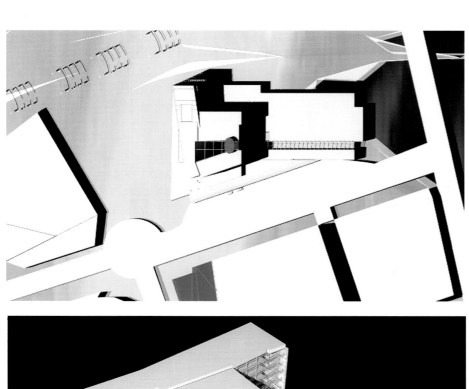

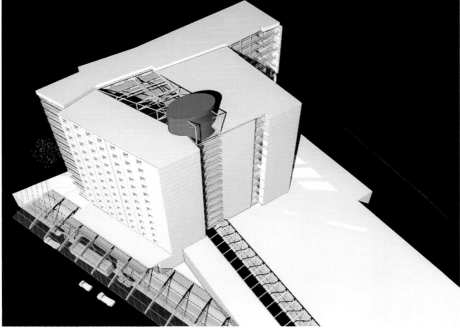

Baron BMW Dealership
Merriam, Kansas

The new Baron BMW Dealership in Merriam, Kansas, is a reinvention of the automobile showroom. During an extensive design workshop process with the design team, the client continued to select options that moved away from the traditional showroom-as-glass-box idea and toward something much more daring and innovative.

The owner and the design team devised the idea of a series of salons instead of one big room. Each salon will feature a single model and be "hosted" by a specialist with in-depth knowledge about that particular vehicle. The team started with one of the trademark BMW showroom features: a roadway. In many showrooms, a straight "road" is delineated into the showroom floor, and the cars are arrayed along it.

But why not curve the road? And why not make it a ramp? A curving "road" ramp is used to form a cylinder—a new take on the glass box. Jutting out from various portions of this smooth curving exterior are jewel boxes that hold one car each, allowing passersby and visitors to read the cars one at a time.

The cylinder, defined by the spiraling road, did not need to be completely transparent, the design team decided; a smooth white porcelain cladding sets the cylinder off as a contemporary, elegant object. The service area and the remainder of the building envelope will be faced with corrugated galvanized metal panels running horizontally, to provide an industrial contrast to the smooth cylinder.

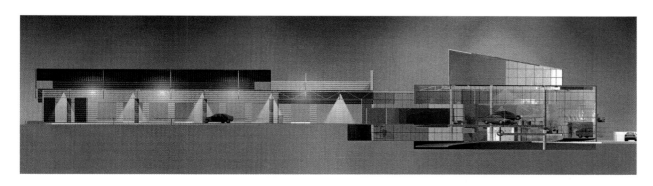

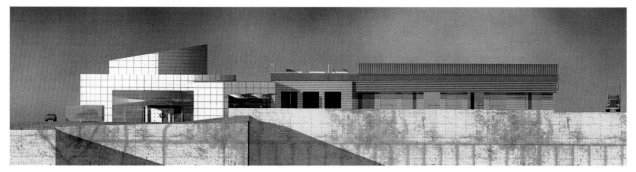

French Creek Corporate Center
Phoenixville, Pennsylvania

In Phoenixville, Pennsylvania, a 130-acre site that was once an iron and steel works is taking shape as an innovative brownfield redevelopment for an office park. Walter Logan of the Delta Organization is planning up to one million square feet of office space in French Creek Corporate Center. The site is centered around the weaving French Creek, alongside which are planned a series of recreation trails. The area is also the center point of the future Schuylkill Valley Metro system, making this project a potential model of sustainable development.

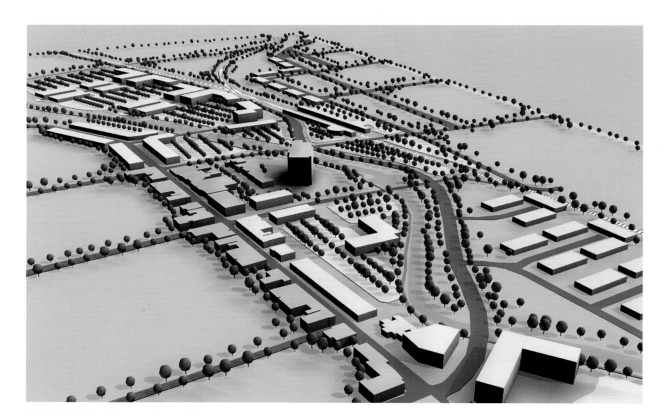

Phoenix Civic Plaza
Phoenix, Arizona

Located in the heart of downtown, Phoenix Civic Plaza plays host to almost two million visitors a year for conventions, trade shows, and civic events. Primary entries are located on the west side of the facility adjacent to a large outdoor public plaza, while the east side is comprised of loading docks. Recent completion of the Arizona History Museum, Arizona Science Center, and Bank One Ballpark are changing the physical and spatial circumstances surrounding Civic Plaza, and public access must evolve in response.

The design challenge is to transform four loading docks into temporary exhibit hall entrances.

The design must conform to loading dock operations and clearances, visually screen loading docks during event mode, require minimal set-up time, require minimal storage, and impact the urban landscape. The design solution redefines threshold by staging an outward reaching spatial experience. Anchors, fabric membranes, and a retractable marquee facilitate the transformation from loading mode to event mode. Anchors are vertical elements that identify entry at the street and serve as structural supports for the fabric membrane system. Clad in perforated metal and precast concrete panels, each anchor houses hoist mechanisms to raise and lower fabric sails. Banner attachments allow vendors flexibility to announce upcoming events, which will contribute to the vitality of the overall urban streetscape.

The fabric membranes serve as elongated screening devices that orchestrate the transition from street to building. Capable of being staged in several hours and requiring minimal storage space, each membrane is shaped to provide the necessary visual screening of adjacent loading docks.

By night, fiber optic lighting located at multiple points on both the anchors and the building will extend its role as a welcoming sign for public entry.

The marquee is comprised of retractable display elements that permanently transform the existing mundane façade and punctuate building threshold. In event mode, it provides vendors flexibility to facilitate multiple banner displays and act as a scaling device upon entry into exhibit halls.

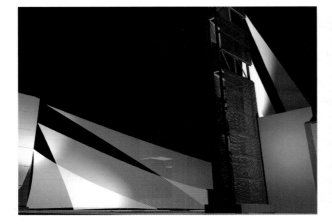

Blue Valley Library
Overland Park, Kansas

The new Blue Valley Library in reflects the evolving definition of "library." Innovations include a pick-up service window, a café, and a gallery wall located along the main corridor. Public areas are organized along a curved "central boulevard" featuring filtered natural daylight and a reading area overlooking a private garden. The garden will feature xeriscaping, requiring little water and maintenance.

A sculptural sun filter in the garden was designed taking into consideration sun rays at various times of day and various times of the year so that it blocks the harshest rays while allowing the maximum daylight into the space that's possible.

Proposal for the Power and Enlightenment Tower
Kansas City, Missouri

As a part of the Kansas City, Missouri, downtown revitalization effort under way, Gould Evans Affiliates teams are working on a series of projects. One of the more speculative plans includes a Proposal for the Power and Enlightenment Tower, conceived as a model for the power and enlightenment for the next millennium. Perched opposite the old Power and Light Tower, a state-of-the-art structure when it was completed in the early part of the century, the new building is intended to push the limits of technology and invention. It would host a community of mixed uses (entertainment, commercial, retail, and residential). The structure would use natural ventilation generated by stack effect and would minimize solar gain based on computer studies of rays and sun strength. Photovoltaic arrays and wind turbines would provide the energy; a wind-powered laser beam would form a gateway with the old Power and Light building, still in use. The facility would include sky courts for communal gatherings and microclimatic Control. The design is based on a computer-generated analysis of downtown Kansas City's urban form, heat radiation patterns, wind patterns, and more.

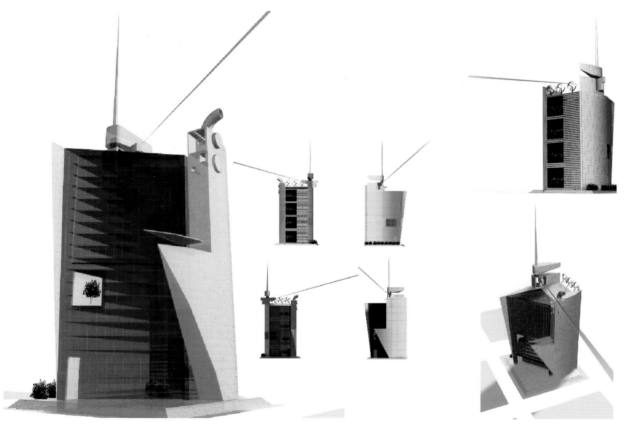

PROJECT CREDITS

J.A. Rogers Middle School
Kansas City, Missouri, 1995
Client: Kansas City, Missouri, School District
Contractor: Walton Construction
Structural Engineers: Leigh & O'Kane
Civil Engineers: Kerr Conrad Graham Associates
Mechanical/Electrical Engineers: M.E. Group, Inc.
Landscape Consultant: McKight Associates, Inc.
Acoustical Consultant: Acoustical
Design Group, Inc.
Food Service Consultant: Judy Ford Stokes &
Associates
Photographer: Mike Sinclair

Center for Health Education
Phoenix, Arizona, 1999
Client: GateWay Community College, Maricopa
County Community College District
Associated Architect: Kahler Slater
Landscape Design: Logan Simpson & Dye
Contractor: JAVCON, Inc.
Construction Management: Abacus Project
Management, Inc.
Structural Engineers: Rudow & Berry Inc.
Mechanical/Electrical Engineers: Baltes/Valentino
& Associates
Civil Engineers: Urban Engineering
LaboratoryConsultant: McLellan & Copenhagen, Inc.
Lighting Consultant: Tim Thomas & Associates
Graphics: Thinking Caps
Photographer: Bill Timmerman

Central Resource Library
Overland Park, Kansas, 1995
Client: Johnson County Library System
Contractor: Jenkins & Associates
Structural Engineers: Bob D. Campbell & Co.
Mechanical/Electrical Engineers: Massaglia,
Neustrom Bredson, Inc.
Civil Engineers: Shafer, Kline & Warren PA
Graphics Consultant: Redline Design Consultants
Lighting Consultant: Yarnell Associates
Acoustical Consultant: Acoustical
Design Group
Photographer: Mike Sinclair

National Hurricane Center
Miami, Florida, 1995
Client: National Oceanic & Atmospheric
Administration, National Weather Service,
Fluor Daniel
Contractor: Hewitt-Kier Construction, Inc.
*Structural, Civil, and Mechanical/Electrical
Engineers:* Fluor Daniel
Consulting Engineer: Herbert S. Saffir Consulting
Engineer
Photographer: Mike Sinclair

Beth Torah Synagogue
Overland Park, Kansas, 1996
Client: Congregation Beth Torah

Contractor: Winn Senter Construction
Mechanical/Electrical Engineers: W. L. Cassell &
Associates, Inc.
Acoustical Consultant: Coffeen, Fricke & Associates
Structural Engineers: Structural Engineering
Associates
Lighting Consultant: Yarnell Associates
Photographers: Mike Sinclair, Douglas Kahn,
John Gutowski

Cathedral Social Hall
Kansas City, Missouri, 1999
Client: Grace & Holy Trinity Cathedral
Consulting Architect: Taylor MacDougall Burns
Architects
Contractor: David E. Ross Construction Co.
MasonryContractor: Diaz Construction Co., Inc.
Structural Engineers: Charles Page & Associates, Inc.
Mechanical/Electrical Engineers: M.E. Group, Inc.
Civil Engineers: SK Design Group, Inc.
Lighting Consultant: Yarnell Associates
Photographer: Timothy Hursley

Westport Center
Kansas City, Missouri, 1996
Client: Gould Evans Goodman Associates
Contractor: A.L. Huber & Sons
Furniture Consultants: Brian Alexander and
Jeff Reuschel with Haworth
Structural Engineers: Norton & Schmidt Consulting
Engineers
Mechanical/Electrical Engineers: The Fagan
Company
Electrical Consultant: Shaw Electric
Mural Artist: Michael Stack
Audio/Visual Consultant: Natural Images
Lighting Consultant: Yarnell Associates
Reception Structure Assembly: Dave Stewart
Photographer: Mike Sinclair

W. Jack Sanders Justice Center
Overland Park, Kansas, 1996
Client: City of Overland Park, Kansas
Contractor: J.E. Dunn Construction Company
Structural Engineers: Boyd Brown Stude & Cambern
Mechanical/Electrical Engineers: BES Engineers
Photographer: Mike Sinclair

Community Health Facility
Lawrence, Kansas, 1999
Client: City of Lawrence, Kansas;
County of Douglas County, Kansas; Bert Nash
Community Mental Health Center; Lawrence-
Douglas County Health Department; Douglas County
Visiting Nurses Association; Douglas County
Hospice Care
Contractors: DiCarlo Construction Co. and B.A.
Green Construction
Structural Engineers: Bob D. Campbell & Co.
Civil Engineers: LandPlan Engineering
Mechanical/Electrical Engineers: Latimer,

Sommers & Associates, PA
Geotechnical Consultant: John Zey
Lighting Consultant: Yarnell Associates
Photographer: Michael Spillars

Student Services Building
Phoenix, Arizona, 1998
Client: Paradise Valley Community College,
Maricopa County Community College District
Contractor: Norquay, Inc.
Construction Management: Abacus Project
Management
Structural Engineering: Nabar Stanley Brown, Inc.
Mechanical/Plumbing Engineering: Kunka
Engineering, Inc.
Electrical Engineering: Associated Engineering, Inc.
Civil Engineering: Evans, Kuhn & Associates, Inc.
Landscape Consultant: Logan Simpson & Dye
Photographer: Bill Timmerman

Prairie Elementary School
Prairie Village, Kansas, 1993
Client: Shawnee Mission Unified School
District No. 512
Contractor: Miller-Stauch Construction Co., Inc.
Structural Engineers: Bob D. Campbell & Co. and
Fasnacht and Nelson, PC
*Structural, Civil, and Mechanical/Electrical
Engineers:* Fluor Daniel
Food Service Consultant: Santee Becker Associates,
LLC
Acoustical Consultants: Acoustical Design Group,
Inc. and
Photographer: Mike Sinclair

Language and Communication Building
Scottsdale, Arizona, 1998
Client: Scottsdale Community College, Maricopa
County Community College District
Contractor: Cohen Contracting
Construction Management: Pinnacle One
Structural Engineering: Nabar Stanley Brown, Inc.
Mechanical/Plumbing Engineering:
Kunka Engineering
Electrical Engineering: Associated Engineering, Inc.
Civil Engineering: Urban Engineering, Inc.
Landscape Consultant: Logan Simpson & Dye
Acoustical Consultant: Acoustical Design Group, Inc.
Photographer: Bill Timmerman

Museums at 18th and Vine
Kansas City, Missouri, 1997
Client: City of Kansas City, Missouri
Associated Architects: Group One Architects
and Associated Architects
Contractors: DiCarlo Construction
Company and Courtney Day, Inc.
Exhibit Consultant: Joseph A. Wetzel Associates
Graphics Consultant: Kiku Obata & Company
Structural Engineers: Leigh & O'Kane
Structural Engineers

Civil Engineers: Taliaferro & Browne
Mechanical/Electrical Engineers: W. L. Cassell
& Associates, Inc.
Landscape Consultant: Martha Schwartz, Inc.
Acoustical Consultant: Coffeen Fricke
& Associates, Inc.
Lighting Consultant: Yarnell Associates
Photographer: Mike Sinclair

Unitog Corporate Headquarters
Kansas City, Missouri, 1997
Client: Unitog Inc.
Contractor: J.E. Dunn Construction Company
Structural Engineers: Structural Engineering
Associates
Mechanical/Electrical Engineers: Smith and
Boucher, Inc.
Civil Engineers: SK Design
Surveyors: Shafer, Kline & Warren
Lighting Consultant: Yarnell Associates
Photographer: Mike Sinclair

Overman Student Center
Pittsburg, Kansas, 1995
Client: Pittsburg State University/State of Kansas
Contractor: Crossland Construction Company
Structural Engineer: Structural Engineering
Associates, Inc.
Civil Engineers: Shafer, Kline & Warren, Inc.
Mechanical/Electrical Engineers: W.L. Cassell &
Associates, Inc.
Photographer: Mike Sinclair

School of Education
Pearson Hall
Lawrence, Kansas, 2000
Client: University of Kansas/State of Kansas
Rendering: Bill McBride

Memorial Student Union
Lawrence, Kansas, 1993
Client: State of Kansas/University of Kansas
Contractor: Ferrell Construction Company
Structural/Civil Engineering: Structural Engineering
Associates, Inc.
Mechanical/Electrical Engineering: W. L. Cassell &
Associates, Inc.
Photographer: Mike Sinclair

Administration Building
Plumb Hall Emporia, Kansas, 1992
Client: Emporia State University/State of Kansas
Contractor: Rinner Construction, Inc.
Structural/Civil Engineers: Finney & Turpinseed
Consulting Engineers
Mechanical/Electrical Engineers: Brack & Associates, P.A.
Photographer: Mike Sinclair

School of Mathematics and Computer Science
Snow Hall, University of Kansas
Lawrence, Kansas, 1991

Client: State of Kansas/University of Kansas
Contractor: Rinner Construction
Structural Engineers: Bob D. Campbell & Company
Mechanical/Electrical Engineers: Gessner and Associates
Photographer: Hobart Jackson

School of Journalism
Flint Hall Lawrence, Kansas, 1983
Client: State of Kansas/University of Kansas
Contractor: Douglas Construction Co.
Photographer: Zercher Photography

School of Architecture
Marvin Hall Lawrence, Kansas, 1981
Client: State of Kansas/University of Kansas
Contractor: Douglas Construction Co.
Photographer: Hobart Jackson

Westminster Promenade
Westminster, Colorado, 1998
Client: AMC Theatres, Inc.
Associated Architect: George Smith
Contractor: MBK Construction Limited
Structural Engineers: Norton & Schmidt
Mechanical/Electrical Engineers: Engineers Consortium
Civil Engineers: Martin & Martin
Lighting Consultant: Yarnell Associates
Irrigation Consultant: Alaback Design
Photographer: Mike Sinclair

Pleasure Island
Lake Buena Vista, Florida, 1997
Client: AMC Theatres, Inc.
Theming Consultant: Design International
Construction Managers: MBK Construction Limited
Project Consultant: Disney Imagineering
Structural Engineers: Norton Schmidt & Warden
Civil Engineers: WDQ Design & Engineering
Mechanical/Electrical Engineers: Engineers Consortium
Landscape Consultant: EDSA
Photographer: Steve Swallow

42nd Street Empire Theater New York
New York, 2000
Client: AMC Theatres, Inc.
Associated Architect: BTA Architects
Historic Preservation Consultant to Developer: Beyer Blinder Belle
Contractor: BONS Construction Corp.
Construction Manager: Lehrer McGovern Bovis
Structural Engineers: Ysrael A. Seinuk, PC
Mechanical/Electrical Engineers: Ambrosino, DePinto & Schmieder
Lighting Consultant: Caribiner
Acoustical Consultant: Acoustical Design Group
Kitchen Consultant: Howard Pascoe Associates
Vertical Transportation
Consultant: John A. Van Deusen Associates, Inc.

Exterior Signage Consultant: ArtKraft Strauss Sign Corp.
Code Consultant: JAM Consultants

Arribida
Porto, Portugal, 1997
Client: American Multi-Cinema Theaters
Associated Architects: Sua Kay Architecta, Design International
Developer: Amorim
Construction Management: AFA Plan
Contractor: Kaiser
Mechanical/Electrical Engineers: Engenheiros Associados
Photographer: Helena Cruz

The Forum
Montreal, Quebec, 2000
Client: American Multi-Cinema Theatres
Associated Architects: Sceno-Plus; Pageau Morel; Tolshinsky & Goodz Architects
Architect of Record/Building Shell: DAA/Daniel Arbour et Associes and IBI/Beinhaker Architects
Associated Interior Designers: Burrows Cave
Developer: Canderel
Contractors: Reliance Construction
Structural Engineers: Shector, Barbachi, Shemie
Mechanical/Electrical Engineers: MCW Consultants
Lighting Consultant: Gabriel Design
Exterior Rendering: Sceno-Plus

Renaissance Hotel And Convention Center
Richardson, Texas, 2001
Client: John Q. Hammons Hotels, LP

Baron BMW Dealership
Merriam, Kansas, 2000
Client: Baron Development

French Creek Corporate Center
Phoenixville, Pennsylvania, 2002
Client: The Delta Organization

Phoenix Civic Plaza
Phoenix, Arizona, 1999
Client: City of Phoenix, Arizona
Fabric Consultant: Ishler Design & Engineering Services
Structural Engineers: Rudow + Berry
Lighting Consultant: Associated Engineering Incorporated

Blue Valley Library
Overland Park, Kansas, 2000
Client: Johnson County Library Board

Proposed Power and Enlightenment Tower
Kansas City, Missouri
Client: The Kansas City Power & Light District

Clockwise from bottom right, the Gould Evans Affiliates principals: Robert Gould, Jay Silverberg, Steve Carpenter, John Wilkins Jr., Steve Clark, Trudi Hummel, Glen LeRoy, Scott Stalcup, Cary Goodman, Greg Nook, David Evans, and Becky Hawkins.

The Power of "We"

In this book, when we—Robert Gould and David Evans—refer to "we," we rarely mean the two of us. The artistic and business endeavor that our firm represents has been crafted by a far greater we—a collection of individuals without whom the firm and its work would never have been realized. Gould Evans Affiliates has grown in the last few years to represent the commitment and leadership of 200 individuals. In the firm's first quarter-century, we've worked with more than 500 people. Influences before and beyond the firm have also been critical; these include Clarence Kivett, Terry Richey, Mike Herman and Tom Nelson. We appreciate the efforts of every individual who has made this collection of work possible.

Chris Andersen	Elizabeth Edmonds	Teresa Kingsley	Adriana Rojas
Neal Angrisano	David Evans	Rebecca Kincaid	Derek Rolfe
Chris Armer	Stephanie Feltenberger	Michael Kinsley	Kent Salisbury
Michael Ashley	Lucy Flynn	Tim Kitchens	Jim Schraeder
Robin Austin	Ron Ford	Scott Klaus	Deb Seeman
Travis Bailey	Bill Fowler	Walter Knight	Ashleigh Self
Donna Barry	Debbie Frederiksen	Rich Kniss	Robert Setterburg
Jennifer Basler	Steve Fucello	Dave Knopick	Krista Shepherd
Leo Berkey	Mike Galloway	Sherry Krisman	Tamara Shroll
Rachel Bias	Tim Ganey	Rick Labonte	Jay Silverberg
Jon Birkel	Gary Gardenhire	John Langley	Henry Sipos
Kevin Blalock	Elizabeth Garvin	Glen LeRoy	William Slusher
Timothy Bott	Ryan Gedney	Heather Lewis	Gary Smith
Margaret Bowker	Ron Geren	Jeff Lewis	Melody Smith
Jason Boyer	Cary Goodman	Tyson Leyendecker	Chris Sogas
Tom Brenneis	Karen Gould	Tim Lies	Neil Sommers
Jillian Brophy	Kira L. Gould	Kristine Lindahl	Scott Stalcup
Bart Brown	Robert Gould	Jennifer Little	Adam Sterns
Kip Brown	Wendy Ham	Patrick Magness	Gary Stoddard
Mary Brunner	Barb Haman	Carol Martin	Dennis Strait
Dave Campbell	Stephanie Hamby	Deb McCoy	Bob Swindler
Ron Campbell	Brian Hamilton	Greg McDowell	Chris Talbert
Steve Carpenter	Steve Harrington	Kurt McGrew	Marcus Thomas
Kevin Carr	Michael Hauser	Melinda Michael	Marilee Thomson
Cindy Childers	Becky Hawkins	Kim Miller	Gina Tleel
Jeffrey Christian	Philip Heelan	Brian Mirakian	Matthew VanBecelaere
Tana Cimino	Michelle Heide	Tammy Montgomery	Matthew Veasman
Jackson Clark	Justin Heigele	Dave Moore	Steve Vukelich
Steve Clark	Steve Heilman	Becky Mullins	Sam Wagner
Linda Clarke	Barbara Hendricks	Scott Neet	Corey Walker
John Cooper	David Herron	Laura Nies	John Ware
Jeremy Crabb	Mindy Highfill	Greg Nook	Kim Washburn
Kristin Crain	Steve Himes	Scott Olson	Andrea Ways Newman
Shawn Croissant	Mark Howard	Rich Ortmeyer	Robert Whitman
Nicole Crutchfield	Rick Howell	Todd Parker	John Wilkins
Sherry Cunnius	Jane Huesemann	Rhonda Pearlman	Christinia Williams
Christopher Davis	Greg Hugeback	David Peeples	Tanya Wilson
John Davis	Trudi Hummel	Jose Pombo	Christy Wisemore
Nancy Davis	Lance Huston	Bill Pyle	Tim Woofter
Scott Dawald	Natasha Idris	Nik Radovanovic	Kristine Young
John Dimmel	Darrin Ingram	Jonathan Rae	Rebecca Young
Doug Doering	Jaime Jacobs	David Reid	Sean Zaudke
Ray Dory	Cheryl Jolley	Tom Reilly	Dan Zeller
Butch Dougherty	Dean Jordan	Anita Ried	Jeremy Zimmerman
Kelly Dreyer	Carolyn Junge	Jesse Robertson	
Dena Eaton	Shawn Kalmus	Jeannie Robinson	
Gloria Edgar	Jeff Kazmaier	Tony Rohr	

Gould Evans Associates
706 Massachusetts Street
Lawrence, Kansas 66044

Gould Evans Goodman Associates
4041 Mill Street
Kansas City, Missouri 64111

Gould Evans Goodman Associates
7201 W. 110th Street, Suite 220
Overland Park, Kansas 66210

Gould Evans Associates
123 Chestnut Street, Suite 203
Philadelphia, Pennsylvania 19106

Gould Evans Associates
5405 Cypress Street, Suite 112
Tampa, Florida 33607

Gould Evans Associates
3136 N. Third Avenue
Phoenix, Arizona 85013

Gould Evans Associates
380 West 800 South, Suite 250
Salt Lake City, Utah 84101

Young Wright /Gould Evans International
172 St. George Street
Toronto, Ontario, Canada M5R 2M7

www.geaf.com